THE
RAGE
AGAINST
GOD

how atheism led me to faith

THE RAGE AGAINST GOD

PETER HITCHENS

ZONDERVAN.com/
AUTHORTRACKER
follow your favorite authors

We want to hear from you. Please send your comments about this book to us in care of zreview@zondervan.com. Thank you.

ZONDERVAN

The Rage Against God
Copyright © 2010 by Peter Hitchens

This title is also available as a Zondervan ebook.
Visit www.zondervan.com/ebooks.

This title is also available in a Zondervan audio edition.
Visit www.zondervan.fm.

Requests for information should be addressed to:

Zondervan, *Grand Rapids, Michigan 49530*

This edition: ISBN 978-0-310-33509-2

The Library of Congress has cataloged the hardcover edition as:

Hitchens, Peter, 1951–
     The rage against God : how atheism led me to faith / Peter Hitchens.
        p.   cm.
     ISBN 978-0-310-32031-9 (hardcover)
     1. Apologetics. 2. Christianity and atheism. 3. Hitchens, Peter, 1951–
    4. Hitchens, Christopher. I. Title.
     BT1103.H58   2010
     239'.7–dc22   2009053282

All Scripture quotations, unless otherwise indicated, are from the Miles Coverdale version of the Bible (1535). Quotations marked KJV are from the King James Version.

Page 72: "On Passing the New Menin Gate," from *Collected Poems of Siegfried Sassoon*, © 1918, 1920 by E. P. Dutton; © 1936, 1946, 1947, 1948 by Siegfried Sassoon. Used by permission of Viking Penguin, a division of Penguin Group (USA) Inc.

Any Internet addresses (websites, blogs, etc.) and telephone numbers in this book are offered as a resource. They are not intended in any way to be or imply an endorsement by Zondervan, nor does Zondervan vouch for the content of these sites and numbers for the life of this book.

Cover design: John Hamilton Design
Interior design: Beth Shagene

Printed in the United States of America

11 12 13 14 15 16 /DCI/ 22 21 20 19 18 17 16 15 14 13 12 11 10 9 8 7 6 5 4 3 2 1

*"Who is this that darkeneth counsel
by words without knowledge?"*

*"Gird up now thy loins like a man;
for I will demand of thee, and answer thou me.
Where wast thou when I laid the foundations of the earth?
Declare, if thou hast understanding."*

*"Who hath laid the measures thereof, if thou knowest?
Or who hath stretched the line upon it?
Whereupon are the foundations thereof fastened?
Or who laid the corner stone thereof?"*

(JOB CHAPTER 38)

Contents

Introduction

*"Thine adversaries roar in the midst
of thy congregations."*
(THE 74TH PSALM)

Only one thing comforts me when I look back at the carnival of adolescent petulance, ingratitude, cruelty, and insensitivity that was my Godless period. I was at least not doing it to fit in with the spirit of the age. I held all my radical positions when they were not yet fashionable, and it was necessary to be quite determined, or perhaps just arrogant, to hold them. I got myself disliked and disapproved of by the very kinds of people who nowadays would be orthodox supporters of "diversity" and secularism, precisely because they are orthodox.

I did what everyone else of my generation was not yet doing. Alas, I still am doing what everyone else in my generation is not yet doing. When I am in church in England now, I notice that it is people of around my age (I was born in 1951) who are mostly absent. There are plenty who are older than seventy or younger than forty, but very few in between. In the United States, I suspect that a great defection of the same kind is now under way in the college generation and that those now in college, or having recently left it, are more hostile — or perhaps worse, indifferent — to religion than any previous American generation. One orthodoxy is giving way to another, as happened in Britain. To explain this, I will have to explain the curious thing that happened to the Christian religion in my country.

In explaining this, I will describe influences I believe have operated on my brother, Christopher, much as they have affected me. It is not for me to say how similar our experiences may have been. We are separate people who, like many siblings, have lived entirely different lives. But since it is obvious that this book arises out of my attempt to debate religion with him, it would be absurd to pretend that much of what I say here is not intended to counter or undermine arguments he has presented in his own book on this subject.

My book, like all such books, is aimed mainly at myself. All polemical authors seek to persuade themselves above all. I hope the book may also be of some value to others, perhaps to believers whose friends or family members have left Christianity or are leaving it now or are enchanted by the arguments of the anti-religious intellects of our age. What I hope to do in the pages that follow is to explain first of all how I, gently brought up in a loving home and diligently instructed by conscientious teachers, should have come to reject so completely what they said. I had some good reasons for refusing some of it. My mistake was to dispense with it all, indiscriminately. I hope to show that one of the things I was schooled in was not, in fact, religion, but a strange and vulnerable counterfeit of it — a counterfeit that can be detected and rejected while yet leaving the genuine truths of Christianity undamaged. That counterfeit still circulates, in several forms, especially in the United States.

I want to explain how I became convinced, by reason and experience, of the necessity and rightness of a form of Christianity that is modest, accommodating, and thoughtful — but ultimately uncompromising about its vital truth. I hope very much that by doing so, I can at least cause those who consider themselves to be atheists to hesitate over their choice. I also hope to provide Christian readers with insights they can use, the better to understand their unbelieving friends and so perhaps to sow some small seeds of doubt in the minds of those friends.

I then intend to address the fundamental failures of three atheistic arguments. Namely, that conflicts fought in the name of religion are always about religion; that it is ultimately possible to know with confidence what is right and what is wrong without acknowledging the existence of God; and that atheist states are not actually atheist. Beyond this, I harbor no ambitions to mount a comprehensive rebuttal of the arguments of such prominent atheists as Professor Richard Dawkins, author of *The God Delusion*, or my brother, Christopher.

I am, of course, concerned especially about Christopher. His passion against God, about which he used to say much less, grew more virulent and confident during the years while I was making my gradual, hesitant way back to the altar-rail. As he has become more certain about the non-existence of God, I have become more certain that we cannot know such a thing in the way that we know anything else, and so must choose whether to believe or not. I think it is better by far to believe. I do not seek to thunder as he does, or to answer fury with fury or scorn with scorn. I do not loathe atheists, as Christopher claims to loathe believers. I am not angered by the failure of atheists to see what appears obvious to me. I understand that they see differently. I do think that they have reasons for their belief, as I have reasons for mine, which are the real foundations of this argument. It is my belief that passions as strong as his are more likely to be countered by the unexpected force of poetry, which can ambush the human heart at any time. I am grateful, even so, for the opportunity to challenge his certainties.

It is also my view that, as with all atheists, Christopher is his own chief opponent. As long as he can convince himself, nobody else will persuade him. As I hope I shall make clear, his arguments are to some extent internally coherent and are a sort of explanation — if not the best explanation — of the world and the universe. Although he often assumes that moral truths are self-evident, attributes purpose to the universe, and swerves dangerously round the problem of conscience — which surely cannot *be* conscience if he is right — he is astonishingly unable to grasp that these assumptions are problems for his argument. This inability closes his mind to a great part of the debate and so makes his atheist faith insuperable for as long as he himself chooses to accept it.

The difficulties of the anti-theists begin when they try to engage with anyone who does not agree with them, when their reaction is often a frustrated rage that the rest of us are so stupid. But what if that is not the problem? Their refusal to accept that others might be as intelligent as they, yet disagree, leads them into many snares.

I tend to sympathize with them. I too have been angry with opponents who required me to re-examine opinions I had embraced more through passion than through reason. I too have felt the unsettling lurch beneath my feet as the solid ground of my belief has shifted. I do not know whether they have also experienced what often follows — namely, a long self-deceiving attempt to ignore or belittle truths that would upset a position in which I had long been comfortable; in some ways even worse, it was a position held by almost everyone I knew, liked, or respected — people who would be shocked and perhaps hostile, mocking, or contemptuous if I gave in to my own reason. But I suspect that they have experienced this form of doubt, and I suspect that the hot and stinging techniques of their argument, the occasional profanity and the persistent impatience and scorn, are as useful to them as they once were to me in fending it off.

And yet in the end, while it may have convinced others, my own use of such techniques did not convince me.

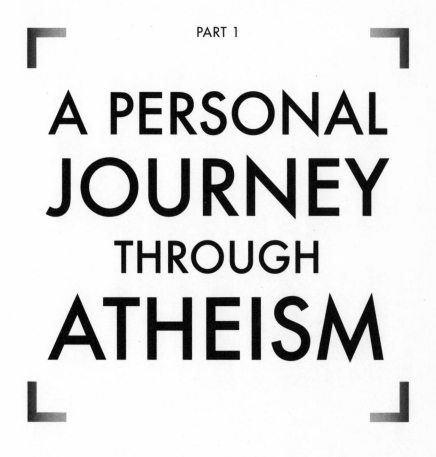

PART 1

A PERSONAL
JOURNEY
THROUGH
ATHEISM

CHAPTER 1

The Generation Who Were Too Clever to Believe

*"Down with it, down with it,
even to the ground."*

(THE 137TH PSALM)

I set fire to my Bible on the playing fields of my Cambridge boarding school one bright, windy spring afternoon in 1967. I was fifteen years old. The book did not, as I had hoped, blaze fiercely and swiftly. Only after much blowing and encouragement did I manage to get it to ignite at all, and I was left with a disagreeable, half-charred mess. Most of my small invited audience drifted away long before I had finished, disappointed by the anticlimax and the pettiness of the thing. Thunder did not mutter. It would be many years before I would feel a slight shiver of unease about my act of desecration. Did I then have any idea of the forces I was trifling with?

I was engaged at the time in a full, perfect, and complete rebellion against everything I had been brought up to believe. Since I had been raised to be an English gentleman, this was quite an involved process. It included behaving more or less like a juvenile delinquent, trying to look like a walking mountain range, using as much foul language as I could find excuse for, mocking the weak (such as a wheelchair-bound boy in my class who provided a specially shameful target for this impulse), insulting my elders, and eventually breaking the law. I haughtily scorned those adults who, out of alarm, concern, love, or duty, sought to warn or restrain me. Nobody can say I did not take my new anti-beliefs to their logical conclusions — hence the decision to finish the job and outrage my religious upbringing by incinerating Holy Writ.

In truth, it was not much of a Bible as Bibles go. It was bound in shiny pale blue boards with twiddly writing on the cover, and it was illustrated with soppy pictures of Christ looking — in C. S. Lewis's potent sneer at stained-glass sentimentality — "like a consumptive girl." Even so, it was the real thing, the proper 1611 Authorized Version, reasonably thumbed by my wide-eyed childish self in scores of Scripture classes, a gift from my parents and until that moment treated with proper reverence and some tenderness. But this was my Year Zero. All that had to go, especially if it had any sentimental associations. We were all free now, and the Bible was one of the things we had to be free of.

At that moment I knew — absolutely knew — that it was the enemy's book, the keystone of the arch I wished to bring down. I knew that there was no God, that the Old Testament was a gruesome series of atrocity stories and fairy tales, while the gospels were a laughable invention used to defraud the simple. And I joyfully and clearly understood the implications of all that, just as W. Somerset Maugham's hero, Philip Carey, understands the meaning of his atheism in the autobiographical novel *Of Human Bondage*, only more so:

> Not knowing that he felt as he did on account of the subtle workings of his inmost nature, he ascribed the certainty he had reached to his own cleverness. He was unduly pleased with himself. With youth's lack of sympathy for an attitude other than its own he despised not a little Weeks and Hayward [fellow students] because they were content with the vague emotion which they called God and would not take the further step which to himself seemed so obvious.
>
> He was free from degrading fears and free from prejudice. He could go his way without the intolerable dread of hellfire. Suddenly he realised that he had lost also that burden of responsibility which made every action of his life a matter of urgent consequence. He could breathe more freely in a lighter air. He was responsible only to himself for the things he did. Freedom! He was his own master at last. From old habit, unconsciously, he thanked God that he no longer believed in Him.

I smugly congratulated myself (as Philip Carey does in this interesting passage) on being able to be virtuous without hope of reward or fear of punishment. I know now that proper virtue is easier to lose, and harder to find, than I thought it was then. I rather think I imagined this was a tremendously original thing to do and a shrewd blow at the dull believers who needed to be scared or bribed into goodness. This is one of the principal joys of the newly fledged atheist, and a continuing joy for many rather experienced non-believers. In this, I was like

Arthur Koestler's peasant who over long years perfects an ingenious invention — a two-wheeled vehicle with a saddle, pedals, and a chain — and then rides it proudly into the city to register the patent, only to discover thousands of people already riding mass-produced bicycles.

But my excitement was undimmed. There were no more external, absolute rules. The supposed foundation of every ordinance, regulation, law, and maxim — from "don't talk after lights-out" and "give way to pedestrians on the crosswalk," to "Thou shalt not commit adultery," "Thou shalt do no murder," "Honor thy father and thy mother," and "Inasmuch as ye have done it unto one of the least of these my brethren, ye have done it unto me" — was a fake. Praying was a comical folly, hymns were so much wailing at an empty heaven, churches were absurd buildings in urgent need of conversion into something more useful, or of demolition. Anyone could write a portentous book and call it Scripture.

Enlightened self-interest was the evolutionary foundation of good behavior. I did not have to do anything that I did not want to do, ever again. I would therefore be "happy," because I was freed from those things whereof my conscience was afraid. My conscience was in any case not to be relied on where my desires were stronger or my fears greater than its promptings. I could behave as I wished, without fear of eternal consequences and (if I was cunning and could get away with it) without fear of earthly ones either. And I could claim to be virtuous too. Unlike Philip Carey, I did immediately recognize that some of the virtues could now be dispensed with, and several of the supposed sins might turn out to be expedient if not actually delightful. I acted accordingly for several important and irrecoverable years.

A Braggart Sinner

That is pretty much as far as my personal confessions will go. My sins are unoriginal. The full details would be tedious for most people, unwelcome to my family (who have enough to put up with anyway), and upsetting for those directly affected by my very worst behavior. Let us just say that they include some political brawling with the police, some unhinged dabbling with illegal drugs (less damaging than I deserved), an arrest — richly merited by my past behavior but actually wrongful — for being in possession of an offensive weapon — very nearly killing someone else (and incidentally myself) through criminal irresponsibility while riding a motorcycle, and numberless acts of minor or major betrayal, ingratitude, disloyalty, dishonor, failure to keep promises and meet obligations, oath-breaking, cowardice, spite, or pure selfishness. I believe that nothing I could now do or say could possibly atone for them.

And then there were the things I thought and wrote and said, the high, jeering tone of my conversation, the cruel revolutionary rubbish I promoted, sometimes all too successfully, with such conviction that I persuaded some others to swallow the same poison. I have more or less recovered. I am not sure they all did. Once you have convinced a fellow-creature of the rightness of a cause, he takes his own direction and lives his own life. It is quite likely that even if you change your mind, he will not change his. Yet you remain at least partly responsible for what he does. Those who write where many read, and speak where many listen, had best be careful what they say. Someone is bound to take them seriously, and it really is no good pretending that you didn't know this.

I should be careful here. Confession can easily turn into showing off one's wickedness. There is a clever H. G. Wells short story about the end of the world called "A Vision of Judgement," in which a grisly tyrant is ordered to own up to his sins at the throne of God. He does so, "white and terrible and proud and strangely noble," much like Milton's Satan in *Paradise Lost*. He turns his confession into a great sonorous boast: "No evil was there but I practiced it, no cruelty wherewith I did not stain my soul ... and so I stand before you meet for your nethermost Hell! Out of your greatness daring no lies, daring no pleas, but telling the truth of my iniquities before all mankind." The braggart sinner's unexpected punishment is to have the true story told, of all his embarrassing private follies, until everyone present is laughing at him and he runs to hide his shame in the Almighty's sleeve. There he finds, crouching next to him, the incendiary prophet who used to denounce him in life, likewise shown up by the recording angel as a laughable fraud, enjoying his outcast status rather too much.

I would add, for those who mistakenly think that religious persons imagine they are better than the rest, that my misbehavior did not stop when I crept stealthily into the pew behind the pillar at the back of the church, where I have skulked for the last twenty-five years. It merely lost its organized, deliberate character. I do not claim to be "saved" by my own declarations or by my attendance at the Lord's Supper. That is up to other authorities, which know my inward heart, to decide.

I talk about my own life at more length than I would normally think right, because I need to explain that I have passed through the same atheist revelation that most self-confident members of my British generation have experienced. We were sure that we, and our civilization, had grown out of the nursery myths of God, angels, and heaven. We had modern medicine, penicillin, jet engines, the welfare state, the United Nations, and "science," which explained everything that needed to be explained. People still died, it was true, but generally off-stage and drugged into a painless passivity. We could not imagine ourselves ever doing so. The "pains of death" had been abolished, along with most of the pains of life.

I was convinced that a grown-up person had no need of Santa Claus fantasies or pies in the sky. I knew all the standard arguments (who does not?) about how Christianity had stolen its myths and feast days from pagan faiths, and was another in a long line of fairy stories about gods who die and rise again. Since all the great faiths disagreed, they couldn't all be right. Jesus was curiously similar to Mithras, or was it Horus? Etcetera, etcetera, etcetera, easy as pie, not in the sky, and made still more facile by the way such youthful epiphanies are applauded by many teachers and other influential adults, and endorsed by the general culture of my country, which views God as a nuisance and religion as an embarrassment or worse.

The Dismissal of Faith by the Intelligent and Educated

The fury and almost physical disgust of the Bloomsbury novelist Virginia Woolf at T. S. Eliot's conversion to Christianity is an open expression of the private feelings of the educated British middle class, normally left unspoken but conveyed by body language or facial expression when the subject of religion cannot be avoided. Mrs. Woolf wrote to her sister in 1928, in terms that perfectly epitomize the enlightened English person's scorn for faith and those who hold it:

> I have had a most shameful and distressing interview with poor dear Tom Eliot, who may be called dead to us all from this day forward. He has become an Anglo-Catholic, believes in God and immortality, and goes to church. I was really shocked. A corpse would seem to me more credible than he is. I mean, there's something obscene in a living person sitting by the fire and believing in God.

Look at these bilious, ill-tempered words: "Shameful, distressing, obscene, dead to us all." There has always seemed to me to be something frantic and enraged about this passage, concealing its real emotion — which I suspect is fear that Eliot, as well as being a greater talent than her, may also be right.

This widely accepted dismissal of faith by the intelligent and educated seemed then to be definitive proof that the thing was a fake, mainly because I wanted such proof. This blatant truth, that we hold opinions because we wish to, and reject them because we wish to, is so obvious that it is too seldom mentioned. I had reasons for wanting that proof. There were, after all, plenty of Christian intellects available if I had desired reassurance that faith and intelligence were compatible. But I dismissed them as obvious dupes, who spoke as they did because it was their professional paid duty to do so.

I had spotted the dry, disillusioned, and apparently disinterested atheism of so many intellectuals, artists, and leaders of our age. I liked their crooked smiles, their knowing worldliness, and their air of finding human credulity amusing. I envied their confidence that we lived in a place where there was no darkness, where death was the end, the dead were gone, and there would be no judgment. It did not then cross my mind that they, like religious apologists, might have any personal reasons for holding to this disbelief. It certainly did not cross my mind that I had any low motives for it. Unlike Christians, atheists have a high opinion of their own virtue.

Vanity Seeks Company

When reciting the Apostles' Creed, I had inwardly misinterpreted the expression "the Quick and the Dead" — in my childish ignorance, I had hoped that I might be one of those quick enough to escape the Judgment. I should add here that, while I grew to understand the real meaning fairly swiftly, the phrase never blossomed fully into life until I heard a doctor matter-of-factly describe the moment when our first child stirred in the womb as "the quickening." But that was in another time entirely, and a long way distant.

I had, like so many other young men and women of my age, been encouraged by parents and teachers (made soft by their own hard childhoods) to believe that I was clever, and so better than my fellows. Such vanity seeks company. If I could become one of them — the clever, dry ones — I could escape from the sports-mad, simple-minded, conventionally dull, commonplace people among whom I seemed to have been abandoned for much of the year.

This again is a confession of a serious failing. I was the child (there is one in every class, every Scout troop, every museum trip) who didn't particularly want to join in with the games or the songs. I really did think of myself in this way, and sometimes still do. As one of the free-thinking and enlightened unbelievers, I would not be condemned to normal life in a suburb or a suit. My life would be an adventure. (So it proved, as it turned out, though different from the adventures I had imagined.) I envied them. I wanted to be one of them. It seemed to me to be the height of being truly grown-up, to be liberated from these tedious, apparently trivial rules and all the duties that went with them.

The Deadly Chill of Ancient Chants and Texts

There were other things too. During a short spell at a cathedral choir school (not as a choirboy, since I sing like a donkey) I had experienced the intense beauty of the ancient Anglican chants, spiraling up into chilly stone vaults at Evensong. This sunset ceremony is the very heart of English Christianity. The prehistoric, mysterious poetry of the Magnificat and the Nunc Dimittis, perhaps a melancholy evening hymn, and the cold, ancient laments and curses of the Psalms, as the unique slow dusk of England gathers outside and inside the echoing, haunted, impossibly old building are extraordinarily potent. If you welcome them, they have an astonishing power to reassure and comfort. If you suspect or mistrust them, they will alarm and repel you like a strong and unwanted magic, something to flee from before it takes hold.

Like hundreds of thousands of English middle-class children, I had attempted to survive sermons by leafing through the technical and administrative bits at the very front and very back of the little red prayer book in the pew. I had wrestled with "The Table to Find Easter," with its cabalistic Golden Numbers, and thought it too much like mathematics to be interesting. I had peered at "The Table of Kindred and Affinity" and wondered innocently what fear lay behind these unyielding prohibitions, most of which were also largely unnecessary. What kind of world had required a long list of the people you weren't allowed to marry? Despite the Freudians, I already realized that I couldn't marry my mother even if I wished to, which I must confess I did not. However far I looked ahead, I could not picture myself marrying my deceased wife's father's mother.

I had enjoyed the "Forms of Prayer to Be Used at Sea," especially the one to be said "Before a Fight at Sea against Any Enemy."

> Stir up thy strength, O Lord, and come and help us.... Take the cause into thine own hand, and judge between us and our enemies.

You could almost hear them being said in strong West Country voices, as the rigging creaked and the slow-matches smoldered and the ship turned toward the foe.

But above all I had discovered — and strongly feared and disliked — the ancient catechism that I had (wrongly) imagined I would one day have to learn by heart and repeat to a bishop — a figure I had seen from a distance, medieval in his miter, his outline clouded by incense. I was actively angry and resentful at the catechism's insistence on rules I had no intention of obeying. By the time I was around twelve, I had a sense, when I encountered this text, of a very old and withered hand reaching out from a dusty tomb-like cavity and seeking to pull me down into its hole forever.

The dark purity of the seventeenth-century language was also disturbing. It was the voice of the dead, speaking as if they were still alive and as if the world had not changed since they died — when I thought I knew that the world was wholly alterable and that the rules changed with the times. Now I am comforted greatly by this voice, welcoming the intervention of my forebears in our lives and their insistent reminder that we do not in fact change at all, that as I am now, so once were they, and as they are now, so shall I be. These, as the sentimental but moving old poem has it, are the prayers your father's father knew, and his father before him. Then I came to fear and dislike this voice so much that I rejoiced to see it being silenced by pestilential modernizers. The words I found myself particularly loathing formed part of the answer to the question: "What is thy duty towards God?" They run: "To submit myself to all my governors, teachers, spiritual pastors and masters: to order myself lowly and reverently to all my betters ... to do my duty in that state of life, unto which it shall please God to call me."

This passage well expresses the thing that the confident, ambitious young person dislikes about religion: its call for submission — submission! — to established authority, and its disturbing implication that others can and will decide what I must be and do.

Our Greatest Fear

Behind the fear of submission lies a whole other set of things that my generation did not wish to acknowledge, the thing we feared perhaps most of all, of following our parents into conformity and suburban living, becoming parents ourselves, mowing lawns, polishing shoes, washing the car. This fear is succinctly described in A. S. Byatt's *The Virgin in the Garden*, a 1978 novel looking back on the early 1950s. A character sneers, "Poor dear Jenny scares him not with severity but with suburbia, the dread of our generation, the teacup, the diaper, the pelmet, the flowery stair-carpet, the click of the latch of the diminutive garden-gate."

It was unimaginable that we, the superior and liberated generation, should be trapped in this banality. The very word "suburb" evoked a mixture of apprehension and scorn. Why did we fear this fate so much? Perhaps it was because they brought us up too kindly, convinced in the post-war age that we should not endure the privation, danger, and strict discipline that they had had to put up with, so we turned arrogant. I certainly did.

Perhaps it was because in the "long 1960s" — which began with TV and rock and roll in the late 1950s, reached their zenith in the great year of self-righteousness in 1968, and continue to this very moment — we sensed that the world had left them behind. They were bewildered and alien in their own land, feeling themselves still to be in their prime, but regarded as impossibly old by us, and increasingly feeling old themselves. They had won the war, but — as we shall see — that war and those who had won it had been discredited. To become like them, to dress like them, speak like them, eat what they ate, and enjoy the music and art they liked was to join the defeated, and to be defeated.

To this day I can remember my feelings of mingled dismay and loss of control over my own life as I purchased the piles of equipment necessary for the care of our first child. It was mostly in hideously colored plastic, for in those servantless days in England, parenthood was deeply unfashionable and mainly indulged in by the poor, which meant modish, well-designed baby equipment did not exist. I felt (correctly as it turned out) that I was being called by irresistible force into a state of life I had not chosen and would never have voluntarily accepted.

I have often thought that the strange popularity of abortion among people who ought to know better has much to do with this sensation of lost control, of being pulled downward into a world of servitude, into becoming our own parents. It is not the doomed baby that the unwilling parents hate (and generally it is the father who is liberated from his responsibilities through abortion and who exerts pressure for it). It is the life they might have to live if the baby is born. Others may have expected and even enjoyed this transformation of themselves into mature and responsible beings. My generation, perhaps because we pitied our mothers and fathers, believed that we could escape it. In fact, we believed that we would be more mature, and more responsible, if we refused to enter into that state of life, unto which it should have pleased God to call us. The oddest thing about this process is that we encountered so little resistance. We had, I think, expected and even hoped to be met with hard, uncompromising argument and rebuke. But authority melted away at a touch and mysteriously indulged us as recompense for our insults and rebellion. It was as if a rebel army had reached the limits of the enemy capital and found the forts and batteries abandoned and the defending soldiers fleeing away. Now I know why it was so easy. Then I thought, wrongly, that our victory was our own doing.

CHAPTER 2

A Loss of Confidence

"The kings of the earth stand up,
and the rulers take counsel together against the Lord."
(THE 2ND PSALM)

The revolt against God was plainly in the very air of early 1960s England, before most of us were even aware of it. I think I now know why. God was associated in our minds with the tottering, enfeebled secular authorities of our country, to whom we had bound ourselves at misty, freezing memorial ceremonies each November.

The Failure and Dishonesty of Public Officials

The authorities were not what they claimed to be. The cool competence and the stoicism were a fraud. The catastrophe of the Suez episode in 1956, when our governing class had tried to behave like imperial rulers in Egypt and had fallen flat upon their faces, had shrunk them and weakened their power to command. The government had sought to abuse (as later governments would also abuse) the semi-sacred incantations of 1940: Egypt's leader, Gamel Abdel Nasser, was a "dictator." Acceding to his demands for control over the Suez Canal was "appeasement." As we have found so often since, these modern villains are not Hitlers, and their ill-armed backward nations are not the Third Reich. Nor are our modern leaders noble or heroic. Secretly colluding with France and Israel to fake a pretext for war, as the British government did in 1956, was hardly Churchillian. Although the full details of this chicanery took years to emerge, the smell was bad, and we were vaguely aware that they had lied rather crudely to us. We were also conscious that they had done so while trying to employ the cult of Churchill with which we were imbued. (More about that in a later chapter.)

This failure and dishonesty sapped and rotted everything and everyone, from the local vicar and the village policeman to the grander figures in the nation. None of them ever had quite the confidence they had possessed before. Some, through strength of character, could still exert authority of their own. Others, who had relied on the institutional force of obedience to the good state, had lost it. Older teachers, who could not be trifled with, were still terrifying persons whose anger could make all the blood in your body drain into your feet with a word of rebuke. But that was because they still carried in themselves the style and manners of a more confident time. Younger ones were just ordinary humans. They had to charm us — or fail.

The change imposed by the Suez catastrophe visibly diminished my own father, because one effect of the defeat was the rapid scrapping of much of the Royal Navy in which he served and the enforced retirement of thousands of officers and men. I can just remember the later parts of the crisis itself, through a haze of five-year-old incomprehension. There was no fuel for our family car, because the blockships sunk in the Suez Canal had held up the oil tankers. As a result, my father had to struggle across Dartmoor in the autumnal winds on a decrepit bicycle, at that time definitely not thought of as fitting transport for an officer and gentleman.

This was a nasty foretaste of much greater indignities to follow. Not long afterward, my father found himself unexpectedly forced to retire from the abruptly shrunken fleet in which he had spent his entire adult life. He had to lay aside his splendid uniform and go off to work in an ordinary office in a civilian suit, far from the sea and the wind that he loved. It was easy to tell he did not much like the change, and nor did I. In those pre-terrorist times, officers in the British armed services still wore their uniforms in public places rather than hiding their occupation, as they do now. And they were proper uniforms — not camouflage overalls, but assemblies of brass and braid more-or-less Victorian in their splendor.

I can recreate in my mind the terrible explosion of jealousy and regret I felt when a schoolfellow's father, who had survived the post-Suez cull, arrived on a visit to our school one winter evening, in the grandeur of a naval commander's rig, greatcoat, gold braid, and epaulettes. He swept into the high eighteenth-century hall looking enormously tall and confident, as he was meant to do. The boy in question had until that moment seemed to me to be insignificant and dull, a bespectacled, silent nobody. But that night I would happily have been him instead of me.

Our school was in those days very emphatically naval. Every one of the chilly dormitory chambers in which we wept silently for our far-off homes, before surrendering to sleep on our hard, iron-framed beds, was named after a great warrior on the seas. I can remember the sequence to this day: Blake, Hawke, Benbow, Rodney, Grenville, Frobisher, Howe, Hardy, Sturdee (the sick bay), and finally — for the senior boys — the greatest of all, Drake and Nelson, saviors of their country from the foreign menace. It strikes me now as interesting that Blake — Oliver Cromwell's "General at Sea" — was excused for his anti-monarchist revolutionary sympathies, in a thoroughly royalist and conservative school, by virtue of having been a fine seadog. Two of my teachers were known by their naval and military rank, one a naval commander, one a captain of marines. We all assumed that the ingeniously sarcastic man in charge of our physical education had been a sergeant-major in the army. Even the headmaster's own apartment, with its interesting personal library (the socialist thrillers of Eric Ambler jostling with Fyodor Dostoevsky) and its fearsome Edwardian bathtub, all brass levers and mysterious valves, bore a wooden plaque commemorating Admiral Lord Samuel Hood.

We were expected to follow in this tradition, if we could, though I was to find out around that time that my eyesight did not meet the exacting standards of Her Majesty's Navy. My school, it was clear, would never name a dormitory after me, and I would not, after all, be perishing nobly at my post in cold northern seas in some future war. My old *Wonder Book of the Navy*, with its stiff pages and ancient illustrations of grinning bluejackets coaling dreadnoughts and ramming shells into the breeches of enormous guns, had specially inspired me with the story of sixteen-year-old Jackie Cornwell, Boy (First Class) aboard HMS *Chester* at the Battle of Jutland. Mortally wounded, he had dutifully stayed by his gun. His captain, Robert Lawson, wrote to Jackie's mother:

> He remained steady at his most exposed post at the gun, waiting for orders. His gun would not bear on the enemy; all but two of the ten crew were killed or wounded, and he was the only one who was in such an exposed position. But he felt he might be needed, and, indeed, he might have been; so he stayed there, standing and waiting, under heavy fire, with just his own brave heart and God's help to support him.

How I had envied him.

But now it was obvious that Jackie Cornwell (who was originally tipped into a nameless mass grave and only later canonized as an official War Hero) would not be needed in the future. In fact, I began to suspect that in my England he might even be jeered at for staying at his post when he should have been jostling for urgent treatment in the sick bay and perhaps saving his life.

I had begun to wonder, with increasing urgency, what I might do instead of joining the navy. During brief spells spent outside the confines of school, where I could see how rackety and exhausted my country was becoming, it was also growing plain to me (though I would never have expressed it so clearly at the time) that I had been brought up for a world that no longer existed. I think I realized this, finally and irrevocably, on the dark, cold January day when they propped a small back-and-white TV on a high shelf in the school dining hall, and we watched on a fuzzy screen the funeral of Sir Winston

Churchill — which was also the funeral of the British Empire —
ending with his coffin being borne into the deep countryside for
burial, on a train hauled by the steam engine bearing his name.
It had been taken out of retirement for the occasion. After it was
all over, the funeral train was brusquely towed back to the depot
by a workaday diesel.

There was to be no more picturesqueness of that sort. A
cheap and second-rate modernity was to replace the decrepit
magnificence we had grown used to. The timetable for the
funeral train's run still exists, noting that it "passed" various
signal boxes and junctions at certain set times (though not mentioning the thousands of people who somehow knew that they
ought to line the track in the January chill). Read aloud, so that
"passed" sounds the same as "past," the timetable is a sort of
elegy on rails, as the body-bag of Imperial England is zipped up
ready for final disposal.

Moral Decay —
At a Distance and Close Up

This loss of confidence, combined with the knowledge that I
could not, would not follow in the expected tradition, must have
gone deep. It combined with the effects on me — and everyone I knew — of the Profumo Affair, Britain's great political sex
scandal. This was the moment when the ruling class that had
failed morally and martially at Suez failed in another equally
morally important way, as they perched lubriciously around a
country-house swimming pool. How odd it all seemed to me
as I tried to decode the unhelpfully incomplete accounts of the
affair in the newspapers. I was more sexually innocent than it

would nowadays be possible to be and had no idea what had got into all these characters. We used to practice target-shooting in a dusty loft — the smell of gun-oil and lead still brings it readily back to me — and I would imagine myself on the African Veldt or the Western front, a hidden sniper training his sights on the hated foe. What — apart perhaps from driving a steam locomotive — could be more fun? Yet here was John Profumo, the Secretary of State for War (a title now abolished in case it upsets people), a man with access to all the wonderful toys of war, from submarines to tanks, accused of spending his time with ... girls who also dallied with Russian spies. It was incomprehensible when he had so many guns to play with. What could be wrong with the man?

I was barely aware of what was going on — twelve-year-old schoolboys of my class were not then expected to understand what government ministers might have been doing with call girls, even if the headlines could not be kept from us completely. As for osteopaths, Soho drinking clubs, and West Indian gangsters — the other characters and locations in this seedy melodrama — who knew what to make of them? Certainly not I. I had no idea what a call girl was (or an osteopath) and, as I recall, very little curiosity about what they did. The mere idea of a Soho drinking club gave me a headache, as it still does. We were more interested in the fact that the girls had also been associating with Russian diplomats, presumably spies.

This was also the time of the first James Bond films, of SMERSH (the KGB's special murder squad), and of knives concealed in the shoes of Soviet assassins. Spies were easy to understand, though surely it should be our spies sharing women with Russian defense ministers rather than the other way around?

We always won, didn't we? A Russian naval attaché must, by definition, be an emanation of evil. What was a Minister of the Crown doing in such company? Why were the Russians even allowed to maintain such a person in London? By contrast, I rather liked the look of Mandy Rice-Davies, one of the call girls, and I have long treasured her eloquent and timeless dismissal of a politician's denial of his role in the scandal "He would, wouldn't he?" Many, many years later I actually met the naval attaché involved: poor vodka-wrecked Captain Yevgeny Ivanov, a babbling human husk, his memory gone, *his* navy a rusting memory like ours, sinking into his final darkness in a Moscow apartment. So much for the glamour of spies.

While we small boys in our knee-length shorts did not really understand what people such as Christine Keeler and Mandy Rice-Davies were for, we knew that their presence in our national life was a bad sign. We knew it had gone rotten, that what we had been taught to revere had lost its nerve and lost its virtue. How right we were. At that time there was only one boy at my school with divorced parents, a fact we whispered about with mingled smugness and horror. Now it is commonplace to find divorced boarding-school parents. To give some idea of the change that has overtaken us, I should also record my reaction to hearing on a news bulletin that some pop star and his girlfriend were to have a baby out of wedlock. I found this unimaginable, impossible. Weddings came first, babies afterward. This was the natural order. I was convinced the baby would be physically abnormal, and my mother had to talk me gently, if elliptically, out of my distress.

Oddly enough, around the same time as the Profumo Affair, a miniature moral scandal exploded at my school. A popular (as it turned out, too popular) master suddenly disappeared. He had been in the habit of entertaining some of the better-looking twelve- and thirteen-year-olds in his room, playing jazz records, and introducing them, perhaps a little early, to the joys of wine. That, alas, was not all he introduced them to. Somebody talked, as someone always does. Justice — or at least retribution — descended swiftly and silently in the night. One morning he was not there, and his classes were taken by others, without explanation. His name was not mentioned. The local newspaper was not in its wonted place on the table in the hall. Several of the older boys made it their business to get hold of a contraband copy, so we were introduced to the mysterious phrase "indecent assault" for the first time. It would not be mysterious for long.

The change that followed was not slow or gradual, but catastrophic, like an avalanche. Small children now know and use swearwords as punctuation. (Mostly they know no other punctuation.) Sexual acts are openly discussed on mainstream broadcasts and explained in British school classrooms with the aid of bananas and hockey-sticks, and boys not much older than I was then are (unsurprisingly) fathering children. The astonishing swiftness of the change, like the crumbling of an Egyptian mummy to dust as fresh air rushes into the long-sealed tomb chamber, has been one of the features of my life. It suggests that our old morality was sustained only by custom and inertia, not by any deep attachment or understanding, and so had no ability to withstand the sneering assault of the modern age.

What happened to me next was, as I shall contend, entirely normal and usual for a boy of my sort in any age or country. But in this context of decay and collapse, it was far more dangerous and far more prevalent.

CHAPTER 3

The Seeds of Atheism

"Thou hast loved to speak all words
that may do hurt."

(THE 52ND PSALM)

I briskly informed my preparatory school headmaster I was an unbeliever when I was about twelve, which would put it in 1963 or 1964, just after John Profumo and Mandy Rice-Davies had burst into my life and well before Winston Churchill's burial. I do not think I volunteered the declaration. I think he had suspected that something of the kind was fermenting inside me, since I was in many ways the tolerated and indulged school troublemaker, expending his subversive energies on complaining about the food and remodeling the school newspaper. (I am told it took years to recover.)

He asked the question expecting the answer he would get. No doubt he had heard it many times before from bumptious outsiders like me. He avoided argument and made a mild riposte about how the deaths of those I loved might later alter my view, which I scorned at the time but which I never forgot and later found to be accurate. I did nothing about it and made nothing of it for some time afterward, being too busy passing some rather difficult examinations, changing schools, and picking my way clumsily through the dismal swamps of early puberty.

A Failure of Christian Education

Although I was extremely well educated by the standards of 2010, I was hopelessly ill-equipped by the measures my grandfather (an accomplished and fearsome teacher and an uncompromising Baptist) would have applied. In my early teens he would some-times stomp around his living room — where he liked to shave toward midday with bowl, brush, and open razor — deriding my ignorance and mocking the made-up discipline of sociology, which I at one stage claimed to be studying. "What *is* sociology?" he roared derisively, twisting and rolling the silly word on his Hampshire tongue. I knew, alas, that he was quite right.

This was no longer the age of faith, so my Bible knowledge was lamentable when compared with that of boys of my class brought up twenty years before — let alone with that possessed by my Anglican aunt and my Calvinist uncle, both of whom knew the King James Version more or less by heart and read and re-read it regularly.

Some of my older teachers, rigorously schooled in a more serious faith, did their best to instruct us as they had been taught. The classes were still referred to, without embarrass-ment, as "Scripture." Later they would be called "Divinity." Later still, there would be "Religious Education." In modern Britain the young are taught about the religious beliefs of others, as if they were an anthropological peculiarity. While teachers are quite ready to be prescriptive about contraceptives (good) and illegal drugs (acceptable if taken with care), they are generally reluctant to urge Christian belief on any of their charges. Some Roman Catholic schools take a stronger line, and Muslim schools certainly do, but those of the established Church of England cannot be relied upon in such things. In a state-maintained Church of England elementary school close to my home, the religious education class recently consisted of instruction in how to draw a mosque. A private school known to me, strongly Anglican, devoted several classes for ten-year-olds to the functions of imams and rabbis, but none to the rites and ceremonies of the Church of England.

By comparison with this, my Christian education was intensive, purposeful, and single-minded. I still recall classes on St. Paul's travels, which must have been identical to those taught fifty years before, and I cannot get out of my head a mnemonic, itself absurdly Edwardian, which was supposed to fix in my head the route Paul had taken around Asia Minor. "Ass Papa!" it ran, "I Like Dates." The last bit referred, I can still recall, to the cities of Iconium, Lystra, and Derbe. The rest is lost to me, but I am struck by the fact that the teacher expected us to know and remember such details of Holy Scripture as a matter of course.

Too often we were left to our own devices, supposedly "searching the Scriptures," a misguided scheme, based on a fundamental misunderstanding of small boys, that involved pasting Bible quotations in an exercise book while supposedly also looking them up and learning them. We did, in my memory, much more sticking bits of paper in exercise books than reading, let alone learning. But our general familiarity with the Bible would still be astonishing in a child of today.

There can have been very little religion at home. I can hardly recall going to church during the school holidays. We were not a church-going family. But since this was quite normal for our class of persons in the 1950s and 1960s Britain, it never struck me as odd, and I never looked for an explanation. The same was true of my parents' marriage, in the wholly secular Caxton Hall in London. My father had most certainly had a Christian religious upbringing — the boys were brought up Baptist, the girls in the more Protestant part of the Church of England. He was familiar with the liturgy and hymns of the Church of England from his own mother's affiliation and from the Royal Navy's weekly observances at sea. Since then, I have guessed that my mother, whose childhood is a mystery to me but whose mother was partly and unobservantly Jewish, did not have any church background at all and decided to leave her children's religious upbringing to the schools. But she too — especially during her wartime years in the Women's Royal Naval Service — would have picked up enough from public ceremony to be able to cope with the (in those days) numerous occasions when our schools required a basic knowledge of Anglican practice. I do not think my father or my mother were actively hostile to faith. I certainly was not withdrawn from Christian religious instruction, an absolute lawful right for any British child if the parents wish to exercise it. I suspect my parents just felt more comfortable for others to be doing this, given their own childhoods and lack of a common faith. But this lack of religion at home has had an odd but powerful effect on my attitude toward Christmas (and, to a lesser extent, Easter).

Christmas at my West Country boarding school was a long festival of anticipation, pleasing to the senses of taste, hearing, and sight. Once Remembrance Day (also known as Armistice Day) was over, we began to prepare for the still-distant feast. We rehearsed a great Carol Service. We were invited to stir the enormous school Christmas pudding, so large and deep that the smaller boys were in severe danger of falling into its rich mixture of dried fruits and spices. The term ended with various happy festivities, including an exhibition where we could show off the items (often quite intricate) that we had spent the term making in woodwork classes, and a Christmas party of a wonderfully old-fashioned English kind, only really possible in a large country house, filled with games and cake until we were exhausted and sated with sugar. This party was always preceded by a long cold walk in the December gloom while normally dour members of the school staff decorated the normally austere hall.

The next day we caught the train — for me a long journey in that strange, exciting light that floods the skies of England when the sun is low in the sky, ending with the unmixed delight of homecoming after dark, the extraordinary pleasures of a soft bed, privacy, and adults who were not teachers. Christmas Eve and Christmas Day, a few days later, were always an anti-climax after this. To this day I prefer the anticipation of Advent to Christmas itself, and the season is strangely incomplete without a long train journey through a cold landscape. As for Easter, I had to teach myself to observe it when I returned to the faith years later. It never fell during the school term, and although the Easter Story, told at any time, is powerful and haunting, the festival itself had no significance for me except as a time for stuffing myself with chocolate eggs.

Imagery of the Last Judgment was still powerful currency

to us. As I will explain later, its power would return one day to surprise me. One of my teachers — actually by far the best of them — would seek to frighten us into learning by warning us that we would suffer the fate of the Foolish Virgins when the time came for the decisive examinations we had to take at the age of thirteen. For us, the Last Judgment was superseded by the fearsome, unyielding tests that would decide the outcomes (or so we believed) of our entire future lives. Pass, and success and security would be ours. Fail, and we would be lost outsiders. I certainly believed it. There would, so the teacher predicted, be wailing and gnashing of teeth and casting into the outer darkness, thanks to our idleness and sloth. He urged us to keep private notebooks of French vocabulary bearing the title "Fuel for the Lamp," to remind us of what might happen if those notebooks were empty. Recently, as I studied the elaborate carvings of the Wise and Foolish Virgins on the west front of the Cathedral at Berne, I found myself thinking unbidden of French irregular verbs and Latin vocabulary.

Faith in "Science"

The Christian conservatism of my schools did not protect me from the rather Victorian faith in something called "science" that was then very common. Perhaps this is because Christianity was not implied in every action and statement of my teachers, whereas materialist, naturalistic faith was. This faith did not require any great understanding. Mainly, it was just an assumption, a received opinion we all accepted. At the age of fifteen, despite an almost complete inability to learn the most basic parts of the school science curriculum, I was wholly satisfied that evolution by natural selection — which I did not under-stand because it was not thought necessary to explain this holy mystery — fully explained the current shape of the realm of nature.

(These days I know, with complete certainty, that there are a number of things about which I have no idea at all, nor does anyone else. This knowledge would have greatly surprised my fifteen-year-old self.)

I likewise thought — when I was solemnly first introduced to it at the age of thirteen — that "science" had fully explained the motions of the planets, the law of gravity, and the mysteries of time. Anything that had not yet been explained would no doubt soon be discovered. There were no mysteries.

Because we could observe gravity in action, we somehow knew what it was. Nobody then mentioned that its operation, especially in empty space, simply cannot be explained. All was settled. Just learn the Table of Elements, your species, your elementary biology, and your formulae, and that was that. The fact that the "laws" dealt with in this subject are all accounts of what *did* happen, rather than rules about how things *should* happen, was passed over in silence. Why and how were silently but inextricably confused. The use of the majestic word "laws" curiously turned the mind away from speculation about whose laws they might conceivably be or why they might have been made. Science, summed up as the belief that what could not be naturalistically or materialistically explained was not worth talking about, simply appropriated them.

Why then should any reasoning, informed person need the idea of God? What would he have explained that was not known among the Bunsen burners, the jars of acid, and the pickled embryos in brownish fluid, in the Science Block? Perhaps if I had been taught science with a little less confidence and told that these claims were open to argument, I might have been more interested in it. (Though I doubt it. My type of school-boy thought it a little demeaning to be "good at" the useful and workaday subjects.). But I should stress that I was not actually taught these articles of the materialist faith, let alone the arguments that continue to rage around them. I was simply given the impression by adults that these things were the case, and that this was all settled forever.

It was the faith of a faithless age. I had no idea, then, quite why so many of the older generation had set their faces so hard against religious belief. I was quite shocked when I later discovered the true state of affairs. They did not know half the things they claimed to know. Their faith in science was an attempt to replace the Christian faith, ruined by wars and disillusion, with a new all-embracing certainty.

Seeking to Banish Darkness and Death

I also recall a very curious thing, which would later change without my realizing how important it was. During my atheist period, I became an enthusiast for total rationality. I happily embraced the cold, sharp metric and decimal systems, discarding the polished-in-use, apparently irrational but human and friendly customary measures — which my generation was the last in England to learn. In a similar desire for mental tidiness, I sought out and preferred buildings without dark corners or any hint of faith in their shape. I was comforted by the presence of modern cuboid structures, preferably of glass and concrete, in any town. I longed for a world of clean, squared-off structures, places where there was no darkness.

I did not know exactly what I was seeking or avoiding, but it was well described in John Buchan's story *Fullcircle*. A character who lives in a seventeenth-century manor house (as did Buchan himself) muses by his library fire:

> In this kind of house you have the mystery of the elder England. What was Raleigh's phrase? "High thoughts and divine contemplations." The people who built this sort of thing lived closer to another world, and thought bravely of death. It doesn't matter who they were — Crusaders or Elizabethans or Puritans — they all had poetry in them and the heroic and a great unworldliness. They had marvellous spirits, and plenty of joys and triumphs; but they also had their hours of black gloom. Their lives were like our weather — storm and sun. One thing they never feared — death. He walked too near them all their days to be a bogey.

As a small child I had been rather interested in death, in graveyards and tombstones. They were not concealed from me as they would be now. The English parish churches of those days had generally not cleared away their graves, altar tombs, and gravestones and turned their churchyards into tactful gardens. Many smelt sweetly of slow human decay. I had little doubt about what was going on beneath those mounds and stones. I had once found a dead mouse, buried it with a short funeral, and soon afterward morbidly dug it up to see what had happened to the corpse. I have never forgotten the sheer purposeful energy of the fat, gray worms I found and the ravenous speed with which they were working. It was almost violent.

I knew far more about death — as a process — than I knew about sex or swearwords, of which I was almost completely ignorant up to the age of twelve. We recited a gruesome rhyme in the playground — seemingly passed on by a magic process from one generation to another — that began, "Never laugh when a hearse goes by, or you will be the next to die," and went on to describe the process of bodily corruption in appalling detail, most of which I can still remember word for word. Does this still continue? I doubt it. But we thought it all jolly and normal.

Having spent long hours in churches peering at memorial tablets, and having walked through many churchyards past worn and leaning stones and worryingly cracked altar tombs, I immediately understood Pip Pirrip's odd ideas about gravestones at the opening of Charles Dickens's *Great Expectations*, a book that continues to have a near-biblical force for me, especially when I consider my treatment of my parents. The gravestones did indeed seem to possess characters. And I was specially, personally terrified when I first read the scene when the young hero finds himself trapped behind an occupied — and rotten — coffin in the burial vault in J. Meade Falkner's tremendous novel *Moonfleet*. I felt as if the author had personally intended to frighten me.

Strangely, as I entered my teens, I no longer felt that close familiarity with death. On the contrary, I sought to ignore it. I shamefully refused to go to my grandfather's funeral and was wrongly allowed to get away with this dereliction — which I have regretted more with every year that has gone past, as I feel that fierce old man's scorn for the modern world coursing through my own veins and hear with perfect clarity his beautiful Hampshire accent in my imagination. I perhaps made up for this later when I attended the burial of his oldest son, my uncle, also a rigorous Calvinist. This took place amid a deluge of icy rain, under a typically black English summer sky, in a cemetery drearily overlooked by the walls of Portsmouth prison and so waterlogged that the mouth of the grave had to be held open with metal props and planks lest it closed with a giant squelch before the service was over.

The hymns and prayers were pure gloom, calculated to spread despond among the living. A relentless pastor intoned as the coffin was lowered: "Our dear brother here departed now goeth either to Heaven or to Hell. There is no scriptural warrant for the existence of any other place." I have to confess — and I am sure my kind and gently humorous uncle would not mind my saying so — that the occasion was so impossibly miserable that it was very nearly funny. I do not think I could have stood it at all during my godless teens, but the fault would have been in me, not in the ceremony.

In the heat of adolescence, when immortality is most attractive, I actively loathed anything that suggested the existence or presence of death. I now positively preferred a world in which death was distant enough to be a bogey, where tombstones were cleared away against the wall, where any sign of dusk or gloom was always banished by enormous windows of plate glass, sparkling light reflected off pale wood, and night defeated by strong electric lamps. I longed to see churches converted into useful libraries or other secular buildings, having first been scoured clean of every last trace of superstition and ritual. I rejoiced at the destruction or desecration or purging of structures with a religious character. They made me feel uncomfortable and resentful. I had a similar loathing for paintings, sculptures, music, or poetry that used religious idioms. This attitude toward painting, in particular, was to end later in an unexpected way.

My moral positions, in the same way, became fierce opposites of what had always been taught. I regarded marriage as something to be avoided, abortion as a sensible necessity and safeguard, homosexuality as very nearly admirable. I renounced patriotism, too — so completely that I would one day shock myself and my fellow revolutionaries with the chilly logical conclusion of this decision. I began by embracing the silly pro-Soviet pacifism of nuclear disarmament, with its bogus claims of moral superiority over the conventional warmongers. In my last disastrous, obnoxious months at my Cambridge boarding school, I learned how to shock my teachers — from sitting up during chapel prayers, to putting my feet on the seat in front of me in the school theatre, to getting caught breaking into a government nuclear shelter. At the end they were all — perhaps especially the best of them whom I had so completely disappointed — more than glad to see the last of me. At the time I had absolutely no idea that I might have been making any kind of mistake. I was in fact rather pleased with myself. I have come to think that this readiness to live entirely in the present — in which we spare ourselves any self-reproach and fail completely to see ourselves as others see us — is a metaphor for the Godless state, in which we simultaneously ignore the experience and warnings of our past and the unknown, limitless dangers of our future.

CHAPTER 4

The Last Battleships

"He breaketh the bow,
and knappeth the spear in sunder."
(THE 46TH PSALM)

I can easily slip into the self-indulgent luxury of living in the past. I know it is purposeless, wrong, and self-deceiving, since the past is irrecoverably gone. I suspect that I do it now, as many others whose parents have died before they were old must do, in the hope of finding a door into a world where my mother and father are restored to life and youth, and I can explain to them how I have at last grown up, and I can introduce their grandchildren to them. But no such door exists, and I assure myself that I do it for a serious purpose — to remind myself, over and over again, how utterly the world can change in a little time and how readily we forget the good that has been thrown aside along with the bad.

Noble Austerity:
The Britain of My Childhood

What I remember about the Britain of my childhood is an

intensely serious and warlike place: trotting by my father's side down a Devon lane, roofed with the branches of ancient trees, and coming across the remnants of an old tank-trap built against the danger of invasion; seeing the painted signs, still not much faded, pointing to air-raid shelters or emergency fire hydrants; rambling along the pitted runway of an emergency airfield yet to be reclaimed by nature, a few hundred yards from my home; gazing at the gaps in the buildings and the still-unrepaired ruins in the great naval cities I inhabited, and the invariable adult reply to the question, "What's that?" being, "A bombed site."

These days, when I hear military experts using the similar-sounding expression "bomb sight," I am immediately transported to the back seat of a bulbous black car, as I peer through the rain-speckled glass at yet another of these weed-grown spaces, never for a second thinking (as my parents must have) that I was looking at the scene of a death, or of many deaths. None of us had died. We had won the war. It was the Germans who had died, and even then, surely not defenseless women and children in their homes. This is what we thought.

It was somber and rather uplifting to live in this noble austerity. The predominant colors of urban Britain at that time were black and gray, under gray skies. For me, it has never been so beautiful since. I have a recollection of a visit to London, with the bright red buses against the monumental black of the great government offices, thrillingly majestic and symbolizing strength and endurance. Now it has all been cleaned and is very pretty, but the severe grandeur has disappeared with the soot.

It all gave the impression of restraint mixed with power. The people were serious, soberly and formally dressed. They spoke tersely in a serious fashion, a disciplined and contained language that was only allowed to show off in poetry or song. The cityscapes were serious. The voices, of all classes, were serious. Words emerged individually from people's mouths rather than in the slurred stream we are familiar with today. Understatement was so universal that it took me twenty years or more to understand fully some of the rebukes directed at me as a child. We were frequently harshly spoken to by adults and were expected to obey instructions. Yet I also remember a great deal of abiding kindness and gentleness toward small children, especially in people's faces and speech.

The Royal Navy: Power Made Visible

The impression of serious purpose was intensified by the naval background to everything — cranes on the near horizon, the clangor of dockyards, my father coming home in uniform, the casual use of naval slang at home, the old kitbags, the dented and much-traveled black tin trunks, Royal Navy pattern, which I used for taking my clothes to and from boarding school — and something else that will never leave me. In those years we still had the last remnants of an imperial, ocean-going navy, and I do not believe there is anything, apart from a great cathedral, that begins to match the visual power of a warship — its symmetry, elegance, and majesty — especially one alive and hung with flags. I would look up at the steel towers and battlements and skyscraping masts, at the gargantuan armored turrets with their fifteen-inch guns, and long to be part of this vibrating, heroic, pungent monster.

Winston Churchill sought to describe the Dreadnoughts of the Grand Fleet leaving their shore stations for war in 1914 as "like giants bowed in anxious thought," but this is less than the half of it. These were castles that could move, works of popular art and architecture, the very idea of power made visible. George Orwell remarks in *Homage to Catalonia* how the sight of big guns mysteriously lifts the spirit.

The loss of these ships makes the heart sink. I still clearly recall the sultry afternoon in August 1960 when HMS *Vanguard,* our last battleship, was towed to the breakers, where she was to be turned into washing machines and razor blades. I knew as I watched the slow, dreary occasion (she ran aground as if in protest) that it was a day of melancholy, loss, and decline, however much the TV commercials of that unusually dishonest and tawdry era tried to tell me that I was in a cheerful age of progress. I had felt the same when allowed, around the same time, to handle a Golden Sovereign, by then a collector's piece but before 1914 the normal day-to-day currency of my country. We had exchanged this real and valuable thing, with its beautiful engraving of St. George slaying a dragon, for a paper promise. How could that be called progress? The word has made me suspicious ever since.

Like most children in victorious great nations, I had a lively mental picture of how things would look and sound as the shells left the muzzles of our great guns. I had no picture about how it might be if another navy opened fire on ours, or little detailed interest in what a fifteen-inch shell might do to those it struck. For we always won, did we not? Even now, the stench of fuel oil can summon back mental pictures of great dockyards full of such ships to my inward eye. But I also make occasional pilgrimages to sad Portsmouth — generally to tend family graves — and pause on the top of Portsdown Hill to see the hulks of decommissioned destroyers, anchored far up the creek and awaiting the blowtorch, and the emptiness of the dockyard that was once the principal arsenal of empire and is now a memorial to national feebleness and decline.

The Illusion of Safety behind the Sea

The Britain of my childhood was an extraordinarily safe place, or at least so it felt to me. The protecting sea was at the end of every road. "Abroad" was impossibly different and chaotic and to be avoided. I wept, as a seven-year-old child, when I discovered that to visit St. Peter's Cathedral (which I had read about in an encyclopedia and immediately wished to see), I would have to go to Italy, a foreign country. I could not imagine myself having to do such a thing. The same encyclopedia, charmingly dated, presented a picture of a distant world of great heat or great cold, uncomfortable, inconvenient, and smelly, if picturesque, in which people lived rather worrying lives from which I was completely protected.

In my grandfather's house, a living museum of Edwardian England, there were many elaborate brass knickknacks from India, which he delighted in bringing out to show his grandchildren. But these only helped to emphasize the distance between there and here. To me, back then, Indians were people in black-and-white pictures, viewed by the fireside as the kettle whispered on the fireside hob my grandfather still maintained in his dark, Victorian living room, and the chiming clock ticked slowly in the corner, as it always had and as I thought it always would.

The Chinese, also, were creatures a million miles away, picturesque and improbably distant. They were like Mr. Lee Hsing, maker of the model junk (a kind of Chinese ship) that my father brought back in 1930 from the Royal Navy's now-forgotten Wei Hai Wei naval station. I have always imagined Mr. Lee in pigtail, trailing moustaches, mandarin robe, and conical hat. I have Mr. Lee's business card still ("Carpenter, Painter and Sculptor, Manufacturer of High Grade Furniture and Toys, Model Junks of Ningpo and Native styles Made to Order"), jaundiced and creased in the hold of the junk, whose red sails long ago crumbled away, a memento of a lost world separated from us by so much violence and upheaval that it is beyond my imagination to conceive of it — not least because I have been many times to modern China and grieved in that devastated, stripped, concrete-blighted land for the loss of so much of its past, in return for such a horrible present.

Of all our many homes, as my father followed the navy around the coast and when — beached at last — he sought something else to do, I was fondest of a modest house in the admiral-infested village of Alverstoke, just across the crowded water from Portsmouth. A small park separated us from the seashore, where I watched ocean liners, epitomizing our wealth, and men-of-war, symbolizing our power, hurrying in and out of Portsmouth and Southampton among brisk and lively waves. At night or in thick fog, their enormous sirens moaned across the vast distance, the most evocative sound in the world. I have never, before or since, felt so perfectly secure.

It is almost impossible to express the sense of ordered peace that lingered about the quiet shaded gardens and the roads without traffic, where my parents were happy to let me and my brother wander unsupervised all day, in a confident, solid world where leather, wood, and brass had not been replaced by plastic and chrome, and a thing had to be heavy and British to be good. Even the money in our pockets was reassuring: royalist, ornate, and weighty pennies, sixpences, shillings, and half-crowns with elaborate coats of arms and inscriptions in Latin, many of those coins older even than my grandfather. So were the enormous Victorian fortresses crouching on the hills behind the city, once one of the most heavily fortified on the planet.

My bicycles and toys were robust machines made in England by English workers. Dark green buses with conductors wearing peaked caps would bear us past a favorite toyshop — and the war memorial — to the Gosport Ferry, from which we could view Her Majesty's still substantial navy at rest as we made our way to the enormous department store where, amid the perfectly preserved accents and manners of the 1930s, my mother made her modest purchases and took me and my brother, neatly brushed and tamed, for tea, éclairs, and cream horns served by frilly waitresses. Incredibly, we often passed the then-famous "Mudlarks," a gang of small boys from the slums, no older than I was, who dived and scrabbled, near-naked, in the harbor mud and slime for brown pennies flung to them by passersby.

The Lingering Trappings of Imperial and Industrial Greatness

I lived at the very end of an era that is now as distant and gone as the Lost City of Atlantis. There were modern things about it, but in general it was a very old civilization. London in the 1950s was modern in an old-fashioned way, really a city of the 1920s and 1930s full of smart electric gadgets and Art Deco design, a relic of the times when we had last been the center of great world empire and a leader among nations. The rest of the country was still more or less Edwardian, in many cases Victorian, shaped by the Industrial Revolution and full of soot and steam.

Steam railway locomotives were things of great beauty — accidental works of art, deliberately built in a patriotic spirit, painted in somber but delicious shades of green, panting like tired dragons, displaying their tremendous inward strength during pauses at junctions, as they released deafening, hundred-foot high columns of steam. Best of all, on a winter evening, was the sight of one of these machines coming into the station, its surrounding cloud of steam pink and orange and gold with the reflection of the great fire within. I always stood back, almost afraid it might leap at me or bite.

Sometimes, on quiet gray summer holiday afternoons — and they were astonishingly quiet in the days before constant traffic and the piping of rock music through loudspeakers — I would slip down to a particular station at a set time, buy a platform ticket, and wait for the romantically-named Atlantic Coast Express to whirl past at 80 miles an hour. This was ours — our invention, our majesty on wheels.

Seen at speed, passing through our soft, intimate landscape, surprisingly small yet packed with force and strength, these locomotives perfectly captured our image of ourselves as a country. The engines that took me home from school in those days had resounding patriotic names — named for Royal Air Force squadrons that had fought in the Battle of Britain or for famous ships of the enormous Merchant Navy we then had. Nowadays their unlovely diesel or electric successors are afflicted with sad, bureaucratic nomenclatures. I recently saw one bearing the nameplate "Victim Support," commemorating a semi-official charity that aids the growing multitude of victims of crime — crime that barely existed when I was little. How very different in every way from the Kings, Castles, and Squadrons of my childhood — and from one particular engine called "Winston Churchill," the locomotive that headed the great man's funeral train.

This engine was one of the very few to survive the seemingly gleeful mass destruction — in the course of an extraordinarily short time — of all of these picturesque locomotives. The sudden disappearance of steam from British railways left the air of the cities much clearer and cleaner, and so allowed us to see more clearly how much we had declined. No wonder we took refuge in the belief that our decay and diminished power had been the price of glory.

CHAPTER 5

Britain's Pseudo-Religion and the Cult of Winston Churchill

"For I will not trust in my bow;
it is not my sword that shall help me."

(THE 44TH PSALM)

N ow we come to the very heart of the cult that enthralled us all, especially children. On thousands of walls hung the reproduction of our national deity — the famous Yousuf Karsh photograph of the truculent warrior glowering in a mono-chrome twilight. We all believed (was it true?) that Karsh had achieved this effect by unkindly snatching the Havana cigar from Sir Winston's lips and recording the resulting expression. My Devon preparatory school displayed a different portrait — this time in color, including the famous cigar, probably a lith-ograph of a once-famous 1942 painting of the Great Man by Arthur Pan — adorned with a quotation that well summed up the battle we thought we had just triumphantly won. "We are all of us defending a cause ... the cause of freedom and justice; of the weak against the strong; of law against violence, mercy and tolerance against brutality and iron-bound tyranny." Alas, I now

Winston Churchill

find that this reproduction was originally sold in thousands to raise money for Mrs. Churchill's "Aid for Russia" fund, money that presumably ended up in the hands of Joseph Stalin's lawless, merciless, intolerant, brutal, and iron-bound tyranny.

I possessed for many years a comic-book biography of our Great Leader called "The Happy Warrior," one of thousands of more or less idolatrous publications that concentrated rather heavily on Mr. Churchill's good side. I knew more about his life than I knew about the life of Christ. Winston was our savior. In fact, the generally radical and irreverent historian A. J. P. Taylor famously called him "the Saviour of his Country" in an impulsive — and uncharacteristically laudatory — footnote to his history of twentieth-century England.[1]

As children, echoes might have reached us of various less-than-complimentary memoirs, of suggestions that the old man's mind was going long before he retired, but we were protected from them by our own desire to believe in his superlative greatness. We had won the war, with him at our head. We whizzed

1. *English History: 1914 – 1945*, Vol. 15 of Oxford History of England (Oxford: Clarendon Press, 1965).

around the playgrounds with our arms outstretched, pretending to be Battle of Britain Spitfires and making machine-gun noises as we sent imaginary Germans spiraling to earth. Once again, we had no thought of what that might have been like for them, and we resisted the idea that our own side had suffered losses of its own. What, us shot down? We won the war!

On freezing evenings, in inadequately heated classrooms or workshops and our fingers dabbled with uncooperative glue, we strove to make plastic models of these aeroplanes or of equally gallant British warships — always rather less impressive and disappointingly smaller in reality than in the dramatically colored pictures on the (much too large) boxes in which these toys were misleadingly sold. The contrast between the packaging and the reality was a metaphor for the difference between what we were then taught to believe about the war and what had actually happened — but we would not find that out until much later.

I possessed a red volume called *Men of Glory*, a title that could not be published now, even ironically. It contained several stories of astonishing but genuine heroism, including that of a man who fought on long after he ought to have been dead (thanks to a Japanese sword-thrust) and a particularly nerve-tightening account of the struggle to remove an unexploded bomb from a claustrophobic space in a submarine. I learned later that my future wife had at the same time been studying its female equivalent, called *Women of Glory*. Many years later in Moscow, these titles returned to worry me when we — a group of expatriate journalists and their spouses — had been discussing the way in which the Soviets liked to use what we thought of by then as the outmoded and exaggerated word "glory" in accounts of their wartime heroes. And it came to me with a shock of memory that there had been a time when we, in prosaic, understated Britain, had done exactly the same and had not thought there was anything odd about it. The Soviet parallel would revisit me again and again to unsettle me. Here was another nation in hopeless decline, comforting itself with a long-ago battle in which it claimed to have saved the world from evil.

And then there was Sergeant Pilot Matt Braddock, the great Royal Air Force bomber ace, fervent democrat (he refused a commission), and all-around British hero. For many years — having encountered him in a book for boys called *I Flew with Braddock*, in which his adventures were recounted by his faithful and admiring navigator, George Bourne — I genuinely believed that this person actually lived. He now has a Wikipedia entry, almost as if he had been a real person, but I now know he never existed outside the pages of a weekly comic.

I had heard of something called "The Blitz," in which German Nazis (they were always Nazis, a special kind of human being deserving of death) had killed our women and children by dropping bombs on their homes. I also had some extremely vague and confused ideas about the massacre of Jews by Germany and may actually have thought that we went to war to save those Jews. If so, I was not alone. Many British people now seem to think that this was our actual reason for fighting Germany, and they are surprised when it is pointed out that this was not so.

In any case, I had no doubt at all that Matt Braddock and his fellow pilots were heroic warriors as they unloaded their bombs upon the evil Nazis. In this I was at least partly right, as I now know. I lost what little physical courage I ever had on the day I crashed my motorbike into a lorry carrying pork pies. The collision (entirely my own fault) nearly removed my right foot. This is as close as I have ever come to the real experience of warfare, though as a journalist I have hung about at the edge of various conflicts doing my best to stay well away from the action. I simply do not know how bomber crews found the courage to climb into their aircraft, especially given the sort of deaths they had already seen so many of their comrades die. What I did not then grasp, and now do, is exactly what Matt Braddock's bombs did when they reached their targets. This late discovery ended my worship of Matt Braddock and of his comrades, brave as they certainly were, and unraveled my entire faith in the whole pseudo-religion we once called, "We Won the War."

The Cult of Noble Death

As pseudo-religions go, ours was attractive and elegant, and it contained many decent and godly elements. Its central ceremony was Remembrance Sunday, the Sunday closest to 11th November. This invariably fell at the low point of the winter term, when the soccer fields were thick with mud the color of tea and the consistency of soup, and a leather football in the face could ruin your entire day. Rain hissed incessantly from misty skies, and the far horizons of summer shrank to a small, murky circle around the school buildings. Through foggy windows we could see only fog. Morning took hours to gain the upper hand over night. The afternoon light began to thicken into a cozy dusk soon after lunch. Feet squelched, puddles formed in doorways, and heavy dark blue raincoats (never fully dry) hung in sodden, musty clumps in the corridors. The normal daily smells of fatty mutton and stodgy puddings loitered in the brown-painted corridors all day. Christmas was too far off to illuminate the darkness.

In the very depth of this season of universal, drab-colored gloom we were marched in ranks and files down to the town war memorial, with absurd caps on our heads, for the crowning ritual of the year.

Everyone else, like us, was somberly clad, and the only color — a startling blood red — came from the artificial poppies we all wore to commemorate the flowers that bloomed among the corpses in First World War Flanders. Wreaths fashioned from the same poppies were heaped on the monument. As a vicar in austere black-and-white vestments intoned uncompromisingly Protestant prayers, we kept a silence. Then a quavering bugle blew, and we sang "O God, Our Help in Ages Past," a hymn that seemed to have been carved from granite much like that of the memorial itself. It was a deep evocation of everything we liked about ourselves, an indulgence in melancholy and proud self-restraint. No outsider could possibly have penetrated its English mystery or imagined that we were in fact enjoying ourselves. But we were.

At that point in my life I still imagined that I too might meet my noble, painless imagined fate in a gray ship on gray seas in some cold northern place, preferably dying at the moment of victory, therefore helping to preserve this unfathomable society from harm. I think I may have believed that my sons might one day process to a memorial and sing sad songs in my memory, standing stiffly upright as the rainwater found its way down the back of their necks.

To this day, I cannot attend or watch this event — for it still continues — without a great wrench of the heart. This was what I believed in most, what I was chiefly proud of, who I truly was. Great poets expressed it, usually but not always sentimentally. "Here dead we lie," as A. E. Housman wrote in 1919,

> because we did not choose
> To shame the land from which we sprung.
> Life, to be sure, is nothing much to lose,
> But young men think it is, and we were young.

And in lines that still make me shiver, Edward Thomas described the shocked Easter of 1915, when a dismayed country began to understand the size of the butcher's bill it was then only beginning to pay for entering so blithely into the First World War. He wrote:

> The flowers left thick at nightfall in the wood
> This Eastertide call into mind the men,
> Now far from home, who, with their sweethearts, should
> Have gathered them and will do never again.

It is only after a minute that the phrase "now far from home" has its intended effect.

Shrines — At Home and Abroad

The great cult of noble, patriotic death has its shrines everywhere, thousands and thousands of them. Some are majestic, adorned with statues of soldiers, sailors, and airmen with bowed heads standing at their corners. Some are considerable works of art. One such is the Cenotaph in Whitehall with its simple-seeming but curiously worrying inscription to "The Glorious Dead." The most evocative — a mud-encrusted infantryman forever reading a letter from home — stands on Platform One of Paddington Station in London. This Great Western Railway Memorial is the work of the sculptor Charles Sargeant Jagger, who also executed the astonishing Royal Artillery Memorial in the heart of London. This is one of the very few to portray a dead soldier (his head and trunk covered by a cloak, his booted legs projecting as a real corpse's would), an enormous and extraordinarily honest tribute to what is described in deeply incised lettering as "A Royal Fellowship of Death." This sculpture, so strange and outlandish that almost nobody studies it, is a full-size representation in solid stone of an enormous Howitzer, trained in the general direction of the Archbishop of Canterbury's palace at Lambeth, no doubt unintentionally. Nearby, the much smaller memorial of the Machine Gun Corps pointedly mocks Jagger's heavy grandeur, with the biblical but un-Christian boast, "Saul hath slain his thousands, but David hath slain his tens of thousands," on its plinth. This curious memorial takes the form of a statue of the young shepherd boy David, naked but for a fig leaf, gripping Goliath's abandoned sword. On either side of him are bronze machine-guns, recreated in careful detail, hung with large bronze wreaths. Once again, the structure is so eccentric, un-Christian, and odd that few ever examine it, though millions must pass by it every year.

In the disturbing and melancholy memorial in the pretty garden city of Port Sunlight in the north of England, sculpted bronze children stand among the sculpted bronze soldiers — intended, I believe, to emphasize the belief that our armies were fighting to defend their homes and families. Now, long afterward, they just call to mind the uncomprehending, or half-comprehending, childish grief that must have broken out in so many homes when fathers did not come home.

Some shrines have powerfully moving inscriptions, especially that of the Metropolitan Railway memorial at Baker Street Station:

> The men from the service of the Metropolitan Railway Company whose names are inscribed below were among those who, at the call of King and country, left all that was dear to them, endured hardness, faced danger, and finally passed out of sight of men by the path of duty and self-sacrifice, giving up their own lives that others might live in freedom. Let those who come after see to it that their names be not forgotten.

Other shrines simply list hundreds of names of the dead, or in small villages a dozen or so, all too frequently two or three from the same family. One, a small obelisk in a Devon hamlet, carries the lines from a forgotten patriotic poem of eighty years ago: "Live thou for England. These for England died." Some are stern and minatory, especially one at the fishing port of Fleetwood, which rather waspishly points out that "Principles do not apply themselves."

All these temples of mourning were originally designed to commemorate one war, that of 1914. All of them were adapted later to commemorate at least one more, that of 1939. An increasing number now bear names from later conflicts. Towering cenotaphs, crowned with globes, look out to sea at the great naval ports. The British traveler abroad will generally find, from Bayeux in France to Rangoon in Burma, sad gardens containing the ordered graves of tens of thousands of soldiers who died abroad and were buried — as was then the custom — where they lay. Colossal monuments at Thiepval and Ypres will continue to mark these cemeteries for hundreds of years to come, each bearing the names of thousands upon thousands of the lost.

British religious architecture, far from dying out, continues to exist in this empire of the dead, with its monumental gates, giant shrines, and graceful colonnades and fountains. Not all the survivors approved. Siegfried Sassoon wrote furiously of the Menin Gate at Ypres:

> *Here was the world's worst wound. And here with pride*
> *"Their name liveth for ever," the Gateway claims.*
> *Was ever an immolation so belied*
> *As these intolerably nameless names?*
> *Well might the Dead who struggled in the slime*
> *Rise and deride this sepulchre of crime.*

A different criticism is made in a faintly sacrilegious story about the same gate, written after the Dunkirk disaster, the defeat of the British Army in Europe in 1940, and its evacuation with the loss of all its equipment, transformed by brilliant Churchillian propaganda into an apparent triumph. In a short story written by an artillery officer, John Austin, using the pseudonym "Gun Buster," a small boy is taken by his father to the Menin Gate on a frozen evening sometime during the 1920s. His parent, a survivor of the First World War, is clearly and profoundly moved by the idea that this was a "War to End War."

They watch a Belgian bugler sound "The Last Post" (the beauti-fully melancholic British equivalent of "Taps") as dusk falls. A few years later, the boy — now himself a soldier in the Second World War — uses the monument as an observation post in a 1940 battle with the Germans, who have no scruples about shooting at it and swiftly drive him to a safer vantage point.

Almost all of these memorials are more or less explicitly religious, but some very pointedly so. In the Buckinghamshire town of Beaconsfield the monument (upon which a light burns at night) is adorned with a carving of Christ crucified. Some compared the sacrifice of 1914 – 18 with the sacrifice of Calvary, an understandable if theologically dubious parallel. A memorial panel in my own parish church bears the words "The Great Sac-rifice." This idea, of a repeated Golgotha in the Flanders slime, is expressed in the rather unsettling hymn, "Oh Valiant Hearts," which was in widespread use throughout what used to be the British Empire until relatively recently — though it is now rarely sung:

> *Proudly you gathered, rank on rank, to war*
> *As who had heard God's message from afar;*
> *All you had hoped for, all you had, you gave,*
> *To save mankind — yourselves you scorned to save.*
>
> *Splendid you passed, the great surrender made;*
> *Into the light that nevermore shall fade;*
> *Deep your contentment in that blest abode,*
> *Who wait the last clear trumpet call of God.*
>
> *Long years ago, as earth lay dark and still,*
> *Rose a loud cry upon a lonely hill,*

While in the frailty of our human clay,
Christ, our Redeemer, passed the self same way.

Still stands His Cross from that dread hour to this,
Like some bright star above the dark abyss;
Still, through the veil, the Victor's pitying eyes
Look down to bless our lesser Calvaries.

These were His servants, in His steps they trod,
Following through death the martyred Son of God:
Victor, He rose; victorious too shall rise
They who have drunk His cup of sacrifice.

There is an almost equally disturbing blurring of the boundaries between the eternal and the temporal in the patriotic poem written by Cecil Spring Rice, a British diplomat whose own brother was to die in the Great War. Set to plangent music by Gustav Holst, it has become one of Britain's most frequently sung national hymns, though the middle verse (originally the first verse of an earlier draft) has been largely forgotten and is not, for understandable reasons, included in the church version. I believe it is not widely known in North America, yet the hymn is sometimes sung at an Episcopalian church in Washington, D.C., attended by both British and American military officers on a mid-November Sunday close to the British Remembrance Day:

I vow to thee, my country, all earthly things above,
Entire and whole and perfect, the service of my love;
The love that asks no question, the love that stands
    the test,
That lays upon the altar the dearest and the best;

The love that never falters, the love that pays the price,
The love that makes undaunted the final sacrifice.

I heard my country calling, away across the sea,
Across the waste of waters she calls and calls to me.
Her sword is girded at her side, her helmet on her head,
And round her feet are lying the dying and the dead.
I hear the noise of battle, the thunder of her guns,
I haste to thee my mother, a son among thy sons.

And there's another country, I've heard of long ago,
Most dear to them that love her, most great to them that
   know;
We may not count her armies, we may not see her King;
Her fortress is a faithful heart, her pride is suffering;
And soul by soul and silently her shining bounds increase,
And her ways are ways of gentleness, and all her paths are
   peace.

Since the 2003 invasion of Iraq, when it seems to me that those who love their countries should have asked many more questions than they did, I have not sung the words "the love that asks no questions" when I have met with this hymn.

Most other countries do not have quite the same deep confusion of patriotism and faith. It is true that Julia Ward Howe's "Battle Hymn of the Republic" comes rather close. This is one of those songs that are so familiar that people pay little attention to the often startling words. Some of its verses are no longer sung, and its exhortation to "die to make men free" is usually changed to "live to make men free." There are, of course, many war memorials in the United States, but there are far fewer of them than in Britain, they are more equivocal, they do not tend to stand in such prominent places, and they are not so universal. The Vietnam monument breathes controversy about the aim and anger about the loss. The Korean War memorial seems resentful that the event has been so easily forgotten. The only American memorials comparable in emotional force to the British ones are those in Southern small towns, recalling the lost cause of the Confederacy. The sole sizeable monument to the dead of the 1917 – 18 war that I have seen in the USA stands opposite Union Station in Kansas City, Missouri. Americans who wish to begin to understand the extent of the British commemoration of war should imagine a Vietnam memorial in every town and city in the country, the center of an annual ceremony and parade and for much of the year adorned with fresh wreaths.

There are war memorials in France, dedicated heartbreakingly to "Children of France, dead for the Fatherland," but they have lost much of their power because of the national defeat in 1940. Some British war memorials in France — notably one at Boulogne — became the focus of anti-German demonstrations after 1940 and were blown up by the occupiers. There are war memorials in Germany, but they have even more embarrassments to conceal or evade, and they are neglected or hard to find.

The only country with a comparable cult of heroic death is Russia, or to be strictly accurate, the former Soviet Union. Compared to the Soviets' colossal statuary, Charles Sargeant Jagger's great artillery monument in London seems modest and restrained. The Soviet War Memorial in Treptow Park in Berlin — built on the site of a mass grave — is plainly a mystical site, with its enormous image of a soldier, sword at rest and cradling a rescued child, that is approached through a ceremonial gate and along a funerary avenue lined with great blocks of stone-like sarcophagi, several of them featuring harrowing reliefs of civilians weeping over the loss of homes and breadwinners and adorned with stern quotations from Stalin. Equally numinous is the eternal flame in the Alexander Gardens under the Kremlin walls in Moscow, with its giant fallen flags and helmets of the dead. Even more so is the vast graven image of the motherland at Stalingrad (now Volgograd) and particularly this supposed dialogue between a German and Russian soldier about the battle, inscribed on the battle memorial. The German asks in astonishment, "They are attacking again. Can they be mortal?" And the Soviet soldier replies, in letters picked out in gold leaf, "Yes, we were mortal indeed, and few of us survived, but we all carried out our patriotic duty before Holy Mother Russia."

These words were actually written by a Russian Jewish journalist, Vasily Grossman, author of the long-suppressed novel of the war, *Life and Fate*. But he is not credited with them on the monument, and I am told that official guides still claim that the writer of the words is unknown. It appears that a Jew cannot be acknowledged as the origin of part of Russia's patriotic-religious legend — something to ponder when we consider that it was at Stalingrad that the blow was struck which would eventually bring down the Third Reich and incidentally save what remained of Europe's Jews.

What is the thing that is being worshiped in these places? It may counterfeit the majesty of great churches and imitate their mystery and grandeur. But it is not God. It is an attempt to replace God, an attempt that failed.

Confusing Patriotism
with Christianity

It was the constant presence of the Soviet war cult, while I was living in Moscow in the final months of the USSR, that pushed me into the full realization that I too had been a devotee of a similar thing. The films of my childhood — *The Cruel Sea, In Which We Serve, Reach for the Sky, Sink the Bismark!, The Dambusters* — were breathless celebrations of the belief that also ran through my schooling. "The War," as we always referred to it, had been a heroic period during which our great and brave country fought more or less alone, and with all classes united, against a powerful and wicked enemy — and defeated it, to the benefit of the whole world.

I also suppressed the fact that, from time to time anyway, we had to have allies. I felt, as did Dorothy Sayers in her poem "The English War," that

> *This is the war we always knew....*
> *When no allies are left, no help,*
> *To count upon from alien hands,*
> *No waverers remain to woo,*
> *No more advice to listen to,*
> *And only England stands.*

History does not support this glorious, inwardly glowing idea of a solitary, embattled island kept warm by bully beef sandwiches, strong sweet tea, and its own valor. There were always allies, even if we had to pay them for their trouble. We counted all too much on the help of alien hands even in 1940.

But it was an essential part of the state religion that sustained us for so long.

I do not mean to be disrespectful. In fact, I am not disrespectful. I love Remembrance Day still. It is a noble remembrance of fine soldiers who did their duty with chivalry and courage, and only a dolt could fail to honor them for their unselfishness and devotion. I will be moved till I die by the sacrifices commemorated. I fight back tears — not always successfully — when the bugles call for the dead, the great guns fire, and the silence falls over England. My father, my grandfather, and my mother all wore the King's uniform in the wars of the twentieth century, and many of their schoolfellows did not survive those wars. The more I know about the nature of war, the more I admire the individual courage of those who did indeed leave all that was dear to them, in the belief that principles did not apply themselves and that human hands and lives — theirs — were needed for the task. I suspect that for many of those involved it was a time of heightened and intensified life, during which they lived at a level of consciousness and endeavor that we now barely understand. The poetry they produced was born in the gap between what they hoped for and what they found. Those who came afterward, illusions torn and hacked away, cannot really write poetry at all.

But the wars in which they were asked to die do not, once examined, seem as noble and pure as they did when I first learned about them. And the proper remembering of dead warriors, though right and fitting, is a very different thing from the Christian religion. The Christian church has been powerfully damaged by letting itself be confused with love of country and the making of great wars. Wars — which can only ever be won by ruthless violence — are seldom fought for good reasons, even if such reasons are invented for them afterward. Civilized countries become less civilized when they go to war. And they hardly ever have good outcomes. In fact, I think it safe to say that the two great victorious wars of the twentieth century did more damage to Christianity in my own country than any other single force. The churches were full before 1914, half-empty after 1919, and three-quarters empty after 1945.

I would add that, by all but destroying British Christianity, these wars may come to destroy the spirit of the country. Those who fought so hard to defend Britain against its material enemies did so at a terrible spiritual cost. The memory of the great slaughter of 1914 – 18 was carried back into their daily lives by millions who had set out from quiet homes as gentle, innocent, and kind and returned cynical, brutalized, and used to cruelty. Then it happened again, except that the second time, the mass-murder was inflicted on — and directed against — women and children in their houses. Perhaps worse than the deliberate, scientific killing of civilians was the sad, desperate attempt to pretend to ourselves later that it was right and justified. In this way, the pain and damage were passed on to new generations who had no hand in the killing. War does terrible harm to civilization, to morals, to families, and to innocence. It tramples on patience, gentleness, charity, constancy, and honesty. How strange that we should make it the heart of a national cult. But there are even worse things than war, as so much of the world also knows.

CHAPTER 6

Homo Sovieticus

*"Under the shadow of thy wings shall be my refuge,
until this tyranny be over-past."*

(THE 57TH PSALM)

Everyone else in the cinema was weeping. The film being shown, in a movie theatre in a northern suburb of Moscow, was not a romance or a sentimental drama, but a documentary entitled "We Can't Go On Living Like This." It had been released for distribution only after a fierce argument at the summit of the Communist apparatus still very much in charge of the then Union of Soviet Socialist Republics. This was June 1990, when the Gorbachev revolution was approaching its final crisis. Why were they crying? Because the film openly told the truth that they all knew but had never been able to discuss.

I remember several scenes: the orderly queue of neatly dressed citizens dissolving into a yelling riot when word came down that the vodka ration for that week had been canceled; the hideous prisoners, faces grotesque from habitual evil, being herded in sordid dungeons; the desolate cityscapes of concrete slabs under poisoned skies, the filthy yellow waste trickling from a crooked pipeline into a polluted sea, the excrement-smeared, desecrated ruins of what had once been churches, the corruption, and the unending official lies.

Soviet citizens all knew life was like this. They knew the daily drudgery of finding anything decent to eat. They knew all the sugar had disappeared from the shops because the official anti-alcohol campaign had impelled millions to make their own vodka in the bathtub. They knew that if they wanted anesthetics at the dentist, or antibiotics at the hospital, or co-operation from their child's teacher, or a holiday by the sea, they would need to bribe someone to get them. Even in Moscow, the show city of the Evil Empire, they knew that they dwelt in the suburbs of hell, that in mile after mile of mass-produced housing you would be hard put to find a single family untouched by divorce, that no mother reared her own children, that the schools taught lies, that secret government establishments leaked radiation into air and water. Fresh eggs were an event. "No" meant "How much will you pay me?" Rats were commonplace and played merrily among the trashcans of apartment blocks and in the entrances of railway terminals. Windows were filthy as a matter of course; I never saw a clean one.

While most struggled to survive, a secret elite enjoyed great privileges — special living spaces, special hospitals with Western drugs and equipment, special schools in which their children were well taught in English, special waiting rooms in stations and airports, and special lanes (one ran down the middle of the street on which I lived) along which the Politburo's giant armored limousines roared at 90 miles an hour, shouldering aside anyone who dared get in the way. The elite had privileged access to good food, foreign travel and books, and the groveling servility of the organs of the state, which oppressed the common people and extorted money from them. This society, promoted by its leaders as an egalitarian utopia, was in truth one of the most unequal societies on earth.

The Soviet Paradise

Thanks to the power of hard currency, I lived on the edges of this elite for more than two years. My apartment, officially a typical worker's quarters, was in reality unavailable to anyone bereft of power or influence. It possessed twelve-foot ceilings, oak parquet floors, uplifting views of the Moscow River on one side and the whole panorama of the city on the other. Its staircase did not stink of urine and cabbage, as those of normal blocks did. My neighbors included the Brezhnev family and several senior KGB officials. It exuded power.

One night shortly before the beginning of the first Gulf War, I had been to a late press conference given by Tareq Aziz, then Saddam Hussein's foreign minister. Because of the midnight hour, I had gone there in my car, a Volvo with special yellow license plates that marked me out as a foreign correspondent. I normally used the Metro, hating the angry, ruthless Moscow traffic and the endless attempts of the GAI traffic police to extort extra-big bribes from the rich foreigner, claiming that I had jumped red lights or broken speed limits when I hadn't. That night, the GAI cops tried to wave me down, 200 yards from my building. I was doing nothing wrong and I ignored them, which sometimes worked because they were lazy as well as corrupt. This time it didn't. Unusually diligent, they gave chase and followed me into the courtyard.

They were angry and perhaps drunk. "Your papers!" demanded the slovenly officer. I gave them to him. He tossed them into the slush at my feet, yelling, "How dare you drive past our checkpoint when ordered to stop! And what are you doing in here anyway?" He gestured in the general direction of the Brezhnevs' vast apartment. He plainly thought I had tried to hide from him and was preparing to demand an unusually large bribe, until I said quietly, "I live here." He stiffened and looked suddenly afraid. He picked up my papers. He looked again at my passport, with its residence permit for that address. He stepped back, saluted smartly, mumbled an apology for bothering me, and drove away without another word. This sort of privilege was unavailable at home in England, where even members of the Royal Family were pulled in for speeding. Yet here I was in a society devoted to equality, asserting real rank over an agent of the state.

I saw only the very end of it. Others have described the Soviet Paradise when it was at the midnight of its dark power — which was, interestingly, the time when it probably worked best. If you are going to have a command economy, then it will function most effectively if there is plenty of fear. By the time I arrived in the Soviet capital in the summer of 1990, there was a shortage of fear — to match the shortages of shoes, furniture, gasoline, cigarettes, and beer. But fear was still there in the background. People knew that the old monster could still lash out and destroy. I saw it do so in Lithuania in January 1991, when it made a last frantic attempt to stop the independence movement and blew holes in several people's heads on a snowy, horrible night.[1] Later, the military claimed that those it had shot were victims of traffic accidents — an insulting lie that made the action even more wicked.

Mistrust and Surveillance

Such abuses were part of a huge apparatus of what I can only call inquisitive evil — a self-serving interest in the lives of others that made normal human trust very difficult. The eventual opening of many secret police files in the former East Germany revealed that tens of thousands of citizens had spied on friends and neighbors in return for official favors. This is now generally accepted by everyone as having been the case, but in Moscow when I was there, we were only guessing at the extent of it. The German revelations confirmed the impression I had in Moscow that the Communist state had made a serious effort to replace and supplant such forces as conscience and self-control. It had taken onto itself the responsibilities of God and of believers in God. But its commandments were very different from those of God.

Even I, an insignificant Western reporter, attracted KGB attention before I had even arrived. A smart and attractive middle-aged woman, who spoke perfect English, made herself agreeable to me on the long train journey from Ostend, Belgium, to Moscow, and hired herself to me as my assistant without trying very hard to conceal her real interest. This could be briefly summed up as, "Are you a spy?" After a few weeks, when it was quite clear that this was most unlikely, she abruptly

---

1. I describe this episode more fully in my book *The Broken Compass* (London: Continuum Books, 2009).

disappeared, along with the driver and cleaner she had also arranged for me. Years later, after Communism had collapsed, she reappeared in my life, claiming that she had vanished in order to care for her dying lover, a KGB agent. Even so, the KGB continued to keep an eye on me after she was gone.

My car was rather obviously fitted with a microphone. (The driving mirror fell from its socket the day after the device was installed.) My phone periodically stopped working, and I had to go around to the exchange and hammer on the door until laughing girls — who knew what was going on — leaned out of a high window to tell me it would be working again by the time I was home (which was always the case). My travel outside the city was closely monitored, and even a picnic in the woods outside Moscow was a nightmare of permissions and documents, since those innocent birch forests were crammed with missiles I was not supposed to see. You never knew who might be informing on you. You learned not to mind.

A Harsh and Dangerous Life

Mistrust and surveillance were not the only things that quickly struck me as different about this society. Soviet life, I learned speedily enough, was incredibly harsh and often dangerous. My Russian acquaintances thought my wife and I were ten years younger than we were. We thought they were ten years older than they were.

Life *began* with harshness. Even for the married, the main form of family planning — in a society that had little room for big families — was abortion, legally unrestricted in the post-war USSR as the need for a vast conscript army receded. In 1990, there were 6.46 million abortions in the USSR and 4.85 million live births. Birth itself was an authoritarian ordeal, with the newborns snatched away from their mothers by scowling nurses in tall chefs' hats, tightly wrapped like loaves, and denied breast or bottle until the set time came around. You could spot a maternity hospital by the strings hanging from the windows, bearing pathetic messages of love or need from wives to husbands. Those husbands were forbidden for days to visit their wives or babies and instead lurked, smoking glumly, on the weedy grass beneath the windows, waiting for a chance to catch sight of them.

Once the baby was home, married life quickly included the state as third parent, since salaries were carefully set so that it took two wages to pay for the basics of life. It was virtually unknown for any mother to stay at home to look after her children, who were placed very early in slovenly nurseries where they rarely died of the neglect they received, but were even more rarely given anything resembling a Western mother's loving attention.

For the average citizen it was a life lived at a dismally low level materially, ethically, and culturally. The Soviet Union may have been a great power, but it was a great power that had diverted its resources into the hands of the state, with only the ruling elite spared the resulting dismal privations. Even the few available consumer goods were a risk to their owners. The chief danger in all lives came from badly built Soviet TV sets, famous for their habit of exploding and setting fire to the apartment, usually killing several people. But there were also collapsing balconies — Russian friends would always tut noisily and urge me to come back inside if I ever dared step onto mine — and mysterious holes in the sidewalk into which the elderly might easily tumble and break bones. Children's playgrounds were obstacle courses of unreliable equipment, strewn with broken glass and plentifully equipped with jagged edges. Here we were, in the midst of real, existing socialism.

While tourists and distinguished visitors were taken to the ballet, ordinary male Muscovites (women wouldn't have dared go there) patronized beer-bars so horrible that I could only wonder at the home life of those who used them. You took your own glass — usually a rinsed-out pickle jar — and a handful of brass coins worth a few pennies, along with some dried fish wrapped in old newspaper. You fed your coins into a vending machine, and pale, acid beer dribbled intermittently out of a slimy pipe into your jar. You then went to a high table, slurped your beer (which tasted roughly the way old locomotives smell), and crunched your fish, spitting the bones onto the floor. There was no conversation.

The alternative was to share a bottle of vodka (which could not be resealed once opened) in the street, a choice of evening that often led to the insensible drinkers freezing to death by the road. Special patrols quartered Moscow on winter nights, rescuing such people rather roughly. Those who had been awarded the Order of Lenin (a medal for major achievement) were allowed to go home afterward. Others were stripped of their clothes, flung into cells, prosecuted, fined, and reported to their employers.

I visited one of the special police stations that handled the drunks, and they showed me a dismal museum of the things Russians drank when they could not get vodka. Cheap Soviet after-shave, apparently, was bearable and intoxicating if drunk through cotton waste. A sandwich of black bread and tooth-paste was mildly alcoholic if nothing else could be found. A popular and bitter jest told the story of a conversation in a drinker's home after the state announced a rise in the price of vodka. "Daddy," asks the child with hope in its heart, "will this mean you will drink less?" "No," replies the head of the house-hold, "It means that you will eat less." Compared with this des-perate squalor, the meanest British public house and the most sordid American bar are temples of civilization and intellectual conversation.

A Coarse and Mannerless Society

There were several other features of life in Communist, atheist, humanist Moscow that impressed me, accustomed as I was to the ordered consideration, general culture, and good manners of a rich and stable Protestant Christian society. One was pointed out to me by a visiting descendant of exiles, whose grandpar-ents had fled the city in the days of Lenin. He had even so been brought up in his American home speaking pure, good middle-class Russian, literary and elegant, that sounded, as he said, "like bells." He told me how shocked he was to hear and read the coarse, ugly, slang-infested, and bureaucratic tongue that was now spoken in the city, even by educated professional people, and featured in its newspapers and on public notice boards. It was, he said, plainly a descent.

I was taken aback by a curious aspect of the Metro, Moscow's enormous, never-resting and often workaday underground rail-way. Many of my journeys took place on remote lines or on modern sections, quite without the ornate glamour of the stations the tourists see. Because of the ferocity of the winters, the entrances to the escalators were guarded by heavy, stiff swing doors that were supposed to keep some of the heat in. I noticed that nobody ever held these doors open for those behind. As the habit of holding doors open for others was ingrained in me, I tried to defy this trend. Far from being delighted or impressed by my attempted courtesy, my Russian fellow passengers looked at me suspiciously, as if I were planning to play a trick on them. One even said in satirical tones, "You're obviously not a Russian!"

A similar collapse of manners could be seen when a trolleybus swung into the roadside to pick up passengers. I often used this means of transportation to get home or to voyage through the outer fringes of the capital. If you were well bundled up, it was reasonably easy to withstand the ruthless pushing, elbowing, and fury that erupted every time the creaking, steamed-up vehicle stopped and flapped its doors open. This was a civilized European city, not Africa, but at such moments it was hard to see the difference apart from the temperature.

It is absolutely true — I saw it many times — that traffic stopped dead when rain began to fall, as every driver fetched windshield wipers from their hiding place and leaped out to fit them to their holders. Any wipers left in place while the car was parked would be stolen as a matter of course. Petty theft of unsecured property was universal — and universally accepted as normal.

Yet, if you could penetrate into the small warm world of a Russian kitchen — where close friends and family gathered over smoked fish, black bread, and vodka to talk long into the night — you found an intense, civilized, and courteous society of immensely knowledgeable and well-educated people, quite capable of common decency once they were in a private society controlled and known by themselves. It was not that they were coarse and mannerless themselves. It was that they lived in a coarse and mannerless world, against which it was futile for the lone individual to fight.

I came to the conclusion — and nothing has since shifted it — that enormous and intrusive totalitarian state power, especially combined with militant egalitarianism, is an enemy of civility, of consideration, and even of enlightened self-interest. I also concluded that a high moral standard cannot be reached or maintained unless it is generally accepted and understood by an overwhelming number of people. I have since concluded that a hitherto Christian society that was de-Christianized would also face such problems, because I have seen public discourtesy and incivility spreading rapidly in my own country as Christianity is forgotten. The accelerating decline of civility in Britain, which struck me very hard when I returned there in 1995 after nearly five years in Russia and the USA, has several causes. The rapid vanishing of Christianity from public consciousness and life, as the last fully Christian generation ages and disappears, seems to me to be a major part of it. I do not think I would have been half so shocked by the squalor and rudeness of 1990 Moscow if I had not come from a country where Christian forbearance was still well established. If I had then been able to see the London of 2010, I would have been equally shocked.

A Brush with Desolation

My experience in the Soviet Empire — the squalor, the stink, the harshness, incivility, and desperation — was a long prelude to a much worse brush with desolation. It was December 1992. I was sitting on a heap of cargo in a Russian-built, Russian-piloted transport plane on its way from Nairobi in Kenya to the Somali capital, Mogadishu. I was used to Russian behavior, and this gave me a sort of jaunty confidence. The load, mainly food, was intended for the bureau of a big international news agency. I and my photographer colleague John Downing had hitched a ride.

Mogadishu by this time was no longer a functioning capital. There were no commercial airport, no law, no police, no streetlights, no electricity, no normal telephones, no foreign embassies. Many other things were missing, too, as we were to find out. What I saw in the next few days has no specifically Christian religious message. The people of Mogadishu are Muslims, and my guess is that it would have been even worse if they were not. Their country has been cursed by the repeated interference of global superpowers, more interested in its strategic location than in its society. It just showed me a vision of how fragile our civilizations are, which is why I think it worth mentioning.

At this point in my life I had already returned to Christianity, rather diffidently, having been confirmed into the Church of England about seven years before. My reasons had been profoundly personal, to do with marriage and fatherhood — a cliché of rediscovery that is too obvious and universal, and also too profound, private, and unique to discuss with strangers. I saw no particular connection, at the time of my return to religion, between faith and the shape of society. I imagined it was a matter between me and God. The atheist Soviet Union, where desecration and heroic survival were visible around me, began to alter that perception. Mogadishu accelerated the process. I thought I saw, in its blasted avenues, its private safety and public terror, and its lives ruled by the gun, a possible prophecy of where my own society was headed — though for very different reasons. I still think this.

As with so many of these occasions, I need only to close my eyes and I am there again. The plane banks over the Indian Ocean and sinks rapidly toward the ground. There is the usual confused roar and bumping as we touch down, and powerful braking. The heap on which John and I are sitting, which had slid backward during take-off, now slides rapidly forward. (This is actually rather enjoyable, but I have never been able to take airline safety videos seriously since then.) We come to a halt.

The doors open onto a beautiful and golden late afternoon, with sunset clearly not all that far off. We clamber out, me in my polished black shoes and blue city suit — I have come here, at short notice and with no preparation, from an assignment in Jerusalem. John is better dressed for the occasion in his photographer's bush gear, but encumbered with a gigantic early-model satellite phone (which will prove wholly useless during our entire stay) and the shiny boxes of his trade. Boys about thirteen or fourteen years old crowd around, all with beautiful high-boned Somali faces, asking, "You want bodyguard?" One, plainly a leader, has an AK – 47 with a pale-blue plastic stock. A man from the news agency has arrived to meet his load. He is the only friendly face and the only English-speaking person. "Do we want a bodyguard?" I ask him "Oh, sure," he says. "If you don't have guards, you'll be dead and naked by morning." I notice, at this point, that the sun is dipping rapidly toward the Western horizon.

John and I hire two of the boy bodyguards, using the international sign language of dollar bills. One of our protectors has an unidentifiable car with the upholstery stripped from its seats and no interior trim. (This is a form of transport that I have now grown quite used to, but that was new to me then.) The news agency man says that he is sorry he cannot help us, that his people have no space at all, but we should be able to find something in town. He waves goodbye. I have the impression he is astonished that we should have come here so totally unprepared, perhaps because I am also astonished about this. My newspaper, I think, has delusions of grandeur. When, a few days ago in Tel Aviv, I had dutifully offered to go, it had been an offer made for the sake of form, expecting to be refused, which it was. But someone has changed his mind, and here I am, trapped in Mogadishu by my own attempt to gain kudos without risk. There is going to be risk after all.

We cram ourselves into the car and lurch and jolt past the ruined arrivals terminal and into the city. There are wide avenues made of mud. There seem to be no trees, no shop fronts, no windows. There is a famine, and children not much younger than my bodyguards are dying, as I shall shortly see, in stinking huts and tents not far from me. There is still light, but it will not be for long. We call at various "hotels," which are white-painted concrete but appallingly bleak and dingy. Only desperation would persuade me to stay in one, but even though I am in fact desperate, I cannot. They are full or boarded up or commandeered by unfriendly militias. We turn into a major avenue and are there confronted by one of the most fearsome things I have ever seen.

Drawn up in line ahead, stretching for perhaps half a mile in the level, melancholy light of the setting sun, are dozens of pick-up trucks, each with a heavy machine gun mounted on it

and with eccentrically dressed men, like nightmare rock musi-
cians — some with spectacularly tangled hair, some with black
berets, all with hard, frightening faces — hunched behind the
guns. These are the lawless militiamen of Mogadishu, and they
are leaving town because the US Marines, in the first President
George Bush's last act before he leaves office, are coming to
rescue Somalia from famine and anarchy.

Luckily these militiamen are too busy or preoccupied — or
perhaps have chewed too much khat (the local intoxicating
herb) — even to notice us, and they begin to roll away as we
appear. They will be back in a few months, to mock the mighty
power of the United States with their crude weapons and their
limitless courage. They all know how to die, as we do not.

But still we have nowhere to sleep, no shelter for the night.
Our child guards are bickering. They plainly have no advice or
ideas. We drive, for lack of anything else to do, down street after
street. Were it not for John's reassuring presence and calm, I
should by now be gibbering with fear instead of merely whim-
pering with apprehension. I am numb and desperate and unable
to see how we are going to survive the night. My imagination,
normally fertile, has tactfully shut down. If I could leave, I would
leave. But there is now no way out.

Night in Mogadishu, in which we will be at the mercy of
anyone who cares to threaten us, is fast approaching. And then
it happens — our miracle. John sees, disappearing around a corner, a familiar back. We chase after it. He calls out, and a face
turns. It is an old friend from Sarajevo. Thanks to this unbeliev-
able coincidence, we are reluctantly given places in a compound
with a German TV crew, who quite reasonably object to having
to share their camel stew, water filter, and generator with these

improvident Englishmen, but — having made their disapproval known — let us in. I fall asleep that night, on bare concrete, hopelessly tired after thirty-six hours of travel and panic, with the sound of gunfire and screams in the middle distance, presumably coming from the people who have not found safety.

In the next few days we toured the city and witnessed the majesty of an amphibious operation, with irritable Navy SEALS hiding in the coastal bushes and furious at being spotted and spoken to, and soldiers in landing craft yelling, "Get out of the way!" as their craft surged onto the moonlit shore, exactly where a Pentagon press officer had told the entire press corps to stand. We saw the dying, who were so familiar from TV that it was shockingly without impact, although the stench that comes with famine, and which TV does not transmit, was not so familiar. (I was struck with an absolute certainty that TV does desensitize us to horror, and I have never since believed anyone who argued otherwise.) But above all, we saw the city, still functioning in a barbaric, prehistoric way and run by clans, each controlling its little territory, the only sources of power in a land without a government.

By this time we had acquired a translator, a scholarly and courteous young man whose concern for our safety was touching, given the great risks he ran himself. We became aware of this when we were stopped at a roadblock and our guide was clearly in a state of great fear, sweating visibly and trying not to tremble. Our bodyguards (who were not in the same clan as the translator) did the talking, and we were eventually waved through. When we were a safe distance away, we found out what had been going on. The guards were too interested in the white foreigners to notice that the interpreter was a member of a hated rival clan. He was quite convinced that they would identify him and shoot him. He had seen such things.

What did we see? The road surface had dissolved to mud and rubble. The sidewalks had crumbled. The buildings were all in some way damaged or defaced. There was no traffic as such. Most people were armed, with the unarmed giving way to the lightly armed and the lightly armed giving way to the heavily armed. Society had broken down into the most basic unit of trust and obligation — which in this Muslim culture, with its permissive attitude to the marriage of first cousins, was the clan.

Some sort of economy functioned. The bundles of khat leaves were delivered. Gasoline could be bought from roadside dumps. Meat could be obtained, and sorghum. Our dollars were valid without question. The powerful had satellite phones and TVs, big American or Japanese cars, electricity generators, and water filters, shielded from view behind walls twelve feet high. This was all new to me, but it would not have its full impact until a week later, when I managed to get out of that awful place.

Safely back in London, I was shown old pictures of Mogadishu as it had been a few years before. The lineaments of the great wide avenue where I saw the armed trucks were just discernible. But where I had seen mud, gangs, and wreckage, there were Italian-style pavement cafes, smart cars in orderly lines, a white-gloved policeman directing the traffic, well-dressed and prosperous people passing by, even a telephone box, and of course, modern shops and civilized-looking hotels. This was the familiar world that I was used to, and in a short time it had become the miserable urban desert in which I had rightly feared for my life. I am sure nobody ever set out to get from the one to the other. But they had done so all the same and in a very short time.

Together with the experience of Soviet society, this venture convinced me that my own civilization was infinitely precious and utterly vulnerable and that I was obliged to try to protect it. When you have seen a place from which the whole apparatus of trust, civility, and peace has been stripped, you are conscious as never before of the value of these things — and more curious than ever about their origins, not in wealth or power, but in the mind of man and in the better angels of his nature.

CHAPTER 7

Rediscovering Faith

*"If we have forgotten the Name of our God,
and holden up our hands to any strange god,
shall not God search it out?"*

(THE 44TH PSALM)

Until I lived in Moscow and visited Mogadishu, my rediscovery of faith was mainly a matter of small things. How did it begin? I am not absolutely sure. By the time I was thirty years old, in 1981, I had achieved some material success. I was doing well in my chosen trade, journalism. That is to say, I was on the staff of a national daily newspaper, engaged in writing about a subject that interested me. I met famous and interesting people as a matter of course. I lived in a beautiful and convenient part of London, I was well paid by anyone's standards. I could afford pleasant holidays with my girlfriend — whom I should nowadays call my "partner," since we were not then married — on the European continent, roaming round France on trains and bicycles, exploring Germany and Italy, even venturing to Prague.

Some of these journeys, along with my daily task of writing about the inner workings of Britain's socialist Labour movement and the increasingly unhinged strikes it kept calling, combined to destroy what remained of my teenage socialism, though I was slow to admit this to myself. I had replaced Christianity, and the Churchill cult, with an elaborate socialist worldview — because I had decided that I did not wish to believe in God or in patriotism.

The Loss of Secular Faith

Everyone I knew then seemed to have the same view. I do not think I had daily contact with any religious person — apart from the secretary on my first small-town paper — for about twenty years. I was shocked and (like Virginia Woolf) almost physically disgusted if any acquaintance turned out to believe in God. Now I was discovering that the secular faiths I held were false. I knew, rather too well, that what one believes — and does not believe — is important. I cannot imagine living without any belief of any kind. I was not capable of existing without a coherent view of the universe. But I was suppressing my loss of faith in a Godless universe, and my loss of faith in humanity's ability to achieve justice. My life was devoted largely to pleasure and ambition.

But what were those pleasures? Two of the arts — architecture and music — move me more than any others, not because I know a great deal about them, but because I can feel their influence upon me, almost as if they were speaking to me. I am particularly fond of Philip Larkin's line about "The trees are coming into leaf, like something almost being said,"[1] because this feeling that something is almost but not quite being said

1. "The Trees," by Larkin (1922 – 85).

seizes me when I encounter certain passages of music and certain buildings.

In my thirties I found that what was almost being said seemed to be the thing I had sought to avoid so hard a few years earlier. But I still did not know what it was. I no longer avoided churches. I recognized in the great English cathedrals and in many small parish churches the old unsettling messages. One was the inevitability and certainty of my own death, the other the undoubted fact that my despised forebears were neither crude nor ignorant, but men and women of great skill and engineering genius — a genius not contradicted or blocked by faith, but enhanced by it. The simple beauty of a hammer beam roof or a Norman chancel arch, let alone of the pillars in Durham nave, seems to be quite beyond the architects and builders of our enlightened age.

I simply cannot remember most of this process, though I can work out quite easily how long it was going on. I think my first acquaintance with York Minster, while I was still a student Trotskyist, probably began the process. But I was still noisily, arrogantly atheist and can remember prosing, during a visit to the old Papal Palace in Avignon, about how annoyingly hard it was to find medieval buildings that were not churches or castles. I would guess I was by then at least twenty-eight or twenty-nine.

Fear and the Last Judgment

What I can recall, very sharply indeed, is a visit to the Hotel-Dieu in Beaune, a town my girlfriend and I had gone to mainly in search of the fine food and wines of Burgundy. But we were educated travelers and strayed, guidebook in hand, into the ancient hospital. And there, worth the journey according to the Green Michelin guide, was Rogier van der Weyden's fifteenth-century polyptych *The Last Judgment*.

I scoffed. Another religious painting! Couldn't these people think of anything else to depict? Still scoffing, I peered at the naked figures fleeing toward the pit of hell, out of my usual faintly morbid interest in the alleged terrors of damnation. But this time I gaped, my mouth actually hanging open. These people did not appear remote or from the ancient past; they were my own generation. Because they were naked, they were not imprisoned in their own age by time-bound fashions. On the contrary, their hair and, in an odd way, the set of their faces

Portions of *The Last Judgment* by Rogier van der Weyden/Musée de l'Hôtel-Dieu, Beaune, France.

were entirely in the style of my own time. They were me and the people I knew. One of them — and I have always wondered how the painter thought of it — is actually vomiting with shock and fear at the sound of the Last Trump.

I did not have a "religious experience." Nothing mystical or inexplicable took place — no trance, no swoon, no vision, no voices, no blaze of light. But I had a sudden, strong sense of religion being a thing of the present day, not imprisoned under thick layers of time. A large catalogue of misdeeds, ranging from the embarrassing to the appalling, replayed themselves rapidly in my head. I had absolutely no doubt that I was among the damned, if there were any damned.

And what if there were? How did I know there were not? I did not know. I could not know. Van der Weyden was still earning his fee, nearly 500 years after his death. I had simply no idea that an adult could be frightened, in broad daylight and after a good lunch, by such things. I have always enjoyed scaring myself mildly with the ghost stories of M. R. James, mainly because of the cozy, safe feeling that follows a good fictional fright. You turn the page and close the book, and the horror is safely contained. This epiphany was not like that at all.

No doubt I should be ashamed to confess that fear played a part in my return to religion. I could easily make up some other, more creditable story. But I should be even more ashamed to pretend that fear did not. I have felt proper fear, not very often but enough to know that it is an important gift that helps us to think clearly at moments of danger. I have felt it in peril on the road, when it slowed down my perception of the bucking, tearing, screaming collision into which I had hurled myself, thus enabling me to retain enough presence of mind to shut down the engine of my wrecked motorcycle and turn off the fuel tap in case it caught fire, and then to stumble, badly injured, to the relative safety of the roadside. I have felt it outside a copper mine in Africa, when the car I was in was surrounded by a crowd of enraged, impoverished people who had decided, with some justification, that I was their enemy. There, fear enabled me to stay silent and still until the danger was over, when I very much wanted to cry out in panic or do something desperate (both of which, I am sure, would have led to my death). I have felt it when Soviet soldiers fired on a crowd rather near me, and so I lay flat on my back in the filthy snow, quite untroubled by my ridiculous position because I had concluded, wisely, that being wounded would be much worse than being embarrassed.

But the most important time was when I stood in front of Rogier van der Weyden's great altarpiece and trembled for the things of which my conscience was afraid (and *is* afraid). Fear is good for us and helps us to escape from great dangers. Those who do not feel it are in permanent peril because they cannot see the risks that lie at their feet.

I went away chastened, and the effect has not worn off in nearly three decades. I have been back to look at the painting since then, and it remains a great and powerful work. But it cannot do the same thing to me twice. I am no longer shocked by the realization that I may be judged, because it has ever after been obvious to me. And once again I have concluded that embarrassment was much the lesser of the two evils I faced.

I do not think I acted immediately on this discovery. But a year or so later I faced a private moral dilemma in which fear of doing an evil thing held me back from doing it, for which I remain immeasurably glad. Without Rogier van der Weyden, I might have done that thing.

Rediscovering Christmas and Swearing Great Oaths

At about the same time, I rediscovered Christmas, which I had pretended to dislike for many years. I slipped into a carol service on a winter evening, diffident and anxious not to be seen. I knew perfectly well that I was enjoying it, though I was unwilling to admit it. A few days later, I went to another service, this time with more confidence, and actually sang. I also knew perfectly well that I was losing my faith in politics and my trust in ambition and was urgently in need of something else on which to build the rest of my life.

I am not exactly clear now how this led in a few months to my strong desire — unexpected by me or by my friends, encouraged by my then unbelieving wife-to-be — to be married in church. I genuinely cannot remember. But I can certainly recall the way the words of the Church of England's marriage service awakened thoughts in me that I had long suppressed. I was entering into my inheritance, as a Christian Englishman, as a man, and as a human being. It was the first properly grown-up thing that I had ever done. My adolescence, if not actually over, was at least coming to an end.

The Rector of St. Brides seemed to put some special force into his recital of the 128th Psalm, which promises, "Thy wife shall be as the fruitful vine upon the walls of thine house; thy children like the olive-branches round about thy table. Lo, thus shall the man be blessed that feareth the Lord." I noticed (as I always do) the mention of fear and nodded to myself.

The swearing of great oaths concentrates the mind. So did the baptisms first of my daughter and then of my wife — who, raised as a Marxist atheist, trod another rather different path to the same place. Her christening followed a particularly lovely and robust form, devised in seventeenth-century England for the many who had been denied infant baptism under the rule of Oliver Cromwell and now wanted to enter the church of their fathers. I remember the rather reasonable answer the candidate is asked to give in reply to the enormous question, "Wilt thou then obediently keep God's holy will and commandments, and walk in the same all the days of thy life?"

The required response is, "I will endeavour so to do, God being my helper" — which seems to me to be a realistic promise. And the next thing in the back of the Prayer Book is the old Catechism, which I had dreaded so much as a refractory child but now read with limitless regret and deepening interest. My own confirmation, by contrast, was a miserable modern-language affair with all the poetic force of a driving test, and endured by me in much the same spirit.

The Prodigal Son Returns Too Late

I quickly found that I was going to have to pay immediately (as well as in other, slower ways) for my long rebellion. The church that I remembered had been a dignified body of sonorous prayers, cool and ancient music, and poetic services and ceremonies that would have been recognizable to the first Queen

Elizabeth and to William Shakespeare. During the years I had been away — and not only away but actively hostile — the Bishops had felt the waves of hatred — from people like me — beating against their ancient walls. And they had responded by trying to make their activities more accessible to the worldly.

The services of the Book of Common Prayer along with the King James Bible, on which I had been raised and which still pervade the language and literature of the English-speaking world, were written to be spoken aloud, by countrymen to whom poetry was constantly present and normal in every action, from sowing and reaping to the cutting of hedges and the planing of wood. Because of this, they stand more or less outside ordinary time, as I think they were designed to do.

Thomas Cranmer's Prayer Book has many virtues, one being that it is largely the work of a man who did not have a very high opinion of himself and who filled its pages with pleas for help in the impossible task of being good. He was also a dramatist of some skill. The service of Holy Communion, for instance, is a perpetual reenactment of the night of the Last Supper. This is why — on those rare occasions when it is celebrated on Maundy Thursday — it chills the church building with fear and trembling and, in parts, seems to be written in letters of fire. Outside, not far away, are the Garden of Gethsemane, the chilly night of loss and betrayal, the rooster preparing to crow three times, and the mob already stirring in its sleep for the show trial, the grotesque procession to the gibbet, and the judicial murder.

The services of Morning and Evening Prayer are the last traces of the unceasing monastic cycle of prayer, which once absorbed thousands of monks, day and night, throughout the Christian world. Evensong in particular has a dreamlike quality, at the edge of both sleep and death. As soon as the opening words are spoken, the mind is drawn away from the daily and the ordinary and toward the eternal.

The Prayer Book has another striking feature. It demands penitence as the price of entry to all its ceremonies. The hard passage from the First Epistle of John — "If we say that we have no sin, we deceive ourselves, and the truth is not in us" — is often the first thing spoken. Soon afterward, the general confession requires a public declaration that "We have erred, and strayed from thy ways like lost sheep." There is "no health in us." We are "miserable offenders." These are not easy words to say, if you mean them. This is not because they are archaic or difficult. Most of them are plain English words of one or two syllables, in beautifully crafted sentences with a memorable rhythm. The fact is, many people prefer not to say them, because they do not like to admit that this is so. The church's solution to this unpopularity was to abandon the requirement, replacing it with vague, half-hearted mumblings or — more often — with nothing at all.

Claiming that their proposed new services were an "alternative," waves of newly ordained liberal clergy fanned out from the theological colleges (where liberal teachers had been working away for years) and in a swift and ruthless revolution drove the old Prayer Book from church after church. Anglicans are very accommodating, deferential, generous, and kindly people. Although most of them probably preferred the old to the new, many thought it would be bad manners, or uncharitable, to resist the urgent demands for novelty issued by their vicars. It was quickly clear that there was in truth no alternative. First, there would be an "experiment" with new forms, which was always deemed a success. Then there would perhaps be a period when old and new alternated. Then the old would be relegated to early morning (a concession to the aged) and perhaps the evening. In a few years, 400 years of almost unbroken tradition had been wiped out. What resistance there was had been patronized or ignored, even if it came in the shape of great figures of literature and poetry such as W. H. Auden, who memorably asked "Why spit on your luck?" This was how it was when I returned.

I had asked for this myself, and I accept it as the consequence of my own rebellion. But it does not make the loss any less painful.

A few years ago I was in Dallas, Texas, in some turmoil after having witnessed the execution of a murderer by lethal injection at the prison in Huntsville. With time to spend before catching my plane back to Washington, D.C., I visited the city's Museum of Art and there found myself standing speechless in front of a painting about as different from Rogier van der Weyden's *Last Judgment* as it is possible to imagine. It was a startlingly pessimistic version of *The Prodigal Son* by Thomas Hart Benton. Now, of all the parables, this one had been the most disturbing for me from the moment I encountered it, which I did — as few do now — in the ringing, unforgettable poetry of the King James Version, which fills the mind with vivid pictures. I could not have known, when I first heard that parable, how much it would eventually apply to me with direct personal force, and in how many ways. But it went home, deep and hard, all the same. I almost know it by heart, and cannot pass a beech tree in autumn, with a litter of nuts about it, without the words, "He would fain have filled his belly with the husks that the swine did eat," coming to mind. It is a bitter story, and we are left at the end wondering how the two brothers dealt with each other in the years to come, even though this is not the point of it.

But Benton had made the tale even more sour. His prodigal son is a figure a little like Tom Joad back from prison in John Steinbeck's *The Grapes of Wrath* and from the same era. He has come home too late. Nobody has seen him from afar off and run joyfully to meet him. There will be no forgiveness, no best robe, no ring, no "music and dancing." He stands in his shabby clothes with his poor, roped suitcase. A beaten-up car — the last trace of his squandered wealth — is parked in the background. He is gaping, with his hand to his mouth, at the ruin of the family homestead, ruin caused by his own greed and wastefulness. He looks as if it is just dawning on him that he is stupid and cruel and without hope. The light is failing in a chilly sky beneath wind-ripped, twisted clouds. Instead of a fatted calf, there is a stark, white animal skeleton, the skull horned, lying in the untended grass. We can guess at the grief, resignation, and failure that have overtaken the family and its home during his heedless absence. Who can he blame for it but himself? The desolation is infinite. And as I surveyed the melancholy remnants of my own church, out of which I had petulantly stomped, I felt the same. It was terrible and wrong, but what was I to say? Where had I been when I was needed?

I threw myself, even so, into an effort to halt or reverse the destruction. I think I knew that this was futile, many years too late. But it allowed me to be both in the church and out of it, which at the time was where I needed to be. I bicycled from place to place in search of citadels of the old worship. In one particularly lovely Oxfordshire church, I enquired of a priest — a cozy-looking, well-padded old gentleman — if they ever used the Prayer Book. He stared at me, his eyes hot with dislike. "Never!" he pronounced, and then almost spat out the words "I hate Cranmer's theology of penitence."

This was one of those moments of abrupt realization — rather like the day when a British railway employee responded to a complaint about an especially late train by saying sarcastically, "You think the railways are run for your benefit, don't you?" — when the truth suddenly became clear to me. It was not the language they disliked (though they probably did dislike it too). It was what the words meant. The new, denatured, committee-designed prayers and services were not just ugly, but contained a different message, which was not strong enough or hard enough to satisfy my need to atone.

Word spread around my trade that I was somehow mixed up in church matters. It was embarrassing. I remember one acquaintance, a distinguished foreign correspondent, turning to me in the press room of the Reagan-Gorbachev summit in Washington, D.C., and remarking that he had heard I was going to church. With a look of mingled pity and horror on his face, he asked, "How can you do that?" He plainly felt much as Virginia Woolf had felt toward T. S. Eliot.[2]

I talked to very few people about this and was diffident about mentioning it in anything I wrote. I think it true to say that for many years I was more or less ashamed of confessing to any religious faith at all, except when I felt safe to do so. It is a strange and welcome side-effect of the growing attack on Christianity in British society that I have now completely overcome this. Being Christian is one thing. Fighting for a cause is another, much easier to acknowledge.

2. See pages 23–24.

And so I find myself, skulking behind the pillar at the back, attending a small village church some distance from my home, so small that the authorities have not — yet — put pressure on it to abandon Cranmer's prayers and the King James Bible. We all know we are refugees, awaiting the moment when some ecclesiastical bureaucrat discovers that we are not in step with the times and takes measures to make us conform.

I have seen elsewhere how they proceed: sometimes by salami-slicing the ancient traditions — one vanishing one year, another the next, until all are gone; sometimes by brutal, abrupt decree; sometimes by dividing and ruling congregations. I have more or less accepted that only God knows whether I will die before the old books are finally stamped out, or the other way around. It will be a near-run thing. But I know that, finally released from any regular use, they will continue to live, perhaps more widely than they ever did before, in the minds of men and women. Nobody can stop me from reciting these texts in private, and I believe that they are so enduring and so filled with truth that they will survive as long as any human work.

This small, private battle for poetry and beauty — to which I am still committed — is as nothing compared to the greater conflict that we now face. No doubt it would be easier to fight if we were better armed. But in recent times it has grown clear that in my own country the Christian religion is threatened with a dangerous defeat, by secular forces that have never been so confident. In the United States, where Christianity appears stronger, it is by no means as powerful and secure as it imagines. Why is there such a fury against religion now? Why is it more advanced in Britain than in the USA? I have had good reason to seek the answer to this question, and I have found it where I might have expected to have done if only I had grasped from the start how large are the issues at stake. Only one reliable force stands in the way of the power of the strong over the weak. Only one reliable force forms the foundation of the concept of the rule of law. Only one reliable force restrains the hand of the man of power. And, in an age of power-worship, the Christian religion has become the principal obstacle to the desire of earthly utopians for absolute power.

CHAPTER 8

The Decline of Christianity

*"I myself have seen the ungodly in great power:
and flourishing like a green bay-tree."*

(THE 37TH PSALM)

Western Christianity has undergone several separate reverses and defeats in the modern era. It was permanently divided by the Reformation; it was weakened by the Enlightenment and the bold claims of modern science; it did itself huge damage during modern wars by allowing itself to be recruited to opposing sides. This problem was most harshly stated by Abraham Lincoln in his second inaugural address on March 4, 1865, in which he pointed to the absurdity of both sides in a war seeking the aid of the same God:

> Both read the same Bible and pray to the same God, and each invokes His aid against the other. It may seem strange that any men should dare to ask a just God's assistance in wringing their bread from the sweat of other men's faces, but let us judge not, that we be not judged. The prayers

of both could not be answered. That of neither has been answered fully. The Almighty has His own purposes. "Woe unto the world because of offences; for it must needs be that offences come, but woe to that man by whom the offence cometh."

Lincoln, who seems not to have been a Christian but who knew his Bible better than most believers, was undeniably right — though his target was not the church but the Christian slaveholders. The same absurdity was on display in the First World War, in which soldiers of both sides initiated and enthusiastically joined an unbearably poignant Christmas Truce in 1914, which — had it spread and taken hold — might have ended the whole undertaking. The decline of Christianity, Catholic and Protestant, in Europe, dates from this war, in which the leaders of the national churches gave their support to the warmaking of democratic politicians and so helped to destroy themselves for many years to come.

Recent European wars had been over more quickly and had not brought about such terrible numbers of deaths and maimings. Many priests and pastors performed great acts of personal bravery and sacrifice, bringing comfort to the dying and not shirking terrible danger and privation. But the gospels could not really be made to endorse or excuse the gross mass murder, the rapid loss of all delicacy of language and feeling, everything that had been considered good and fair before; the acres of unburied dead rotting in plain sight until consumed by rats, the resulting growth of mercilessness and brutality at home, thanks to the corruption of men's morals by what they had seen; the devastation of family life and social order.

As the old regimes, one by one, crumbled and sagged, the churches crumbled and sagged with them. Protestant England was particularly troubled after the war was over, because most of its very Protestant churches were unable to permit the prayers for the dead that so many bereaved families would have liked to offer. Spiritualism, with its promise of renewed contact with the departed, briefly flourished because of this, prompting Rudyard Kipling to write his poem "En-Dor," warning the bereaved that they were being cruelly manipulated for gain. But in general the Church of England suffered the decay in authority and the loss of trust and deference that affected every established pillar of English society. People had gone to war for things they completely believed in, and they had been completely betrayed. Promised glory and honor, they had found hideous death, mud, sin, mutilation, rats, and filth. They had, astonishingly, passed through it without any serious mutiny (in the case of the British armies) or collapse in morale. But they knew — and everyone knew — that they had been fooled and that whatever they had fought for had been lost during the squalor of war. Among those who had deceived them were their Christian pastors. Never such innocence again, as Philip Larkin wrote in his poem "MCMXIV" about the last hours of the old England in August 1914:

> Never such innocence,
> Never before or since,
> As changed itself to past
> Without a word — the men
> Leaving the gardens tidy,
> The thousands of marriages

Lasting a little while longer:
Never such innocence again.

Even so, Christianity still survived into the 1930s and into the early 1950s as a considerable if weakened force. Church attendance fell, but was still healthy by the standards of today. The supremacy of the Christian faith was assumed in schools, state and private, and in public life in general. It was affirmed in great national ceremonies, such as the two Coronations of the era — George VI in 1937, and Elizabeth II in 1953. The national broadcaster, the British Broadcasting Corporation, was still unquestionably Christian. Well into the 1950s it broadcast on its main morning news program an uncompromisingly Christian segment entitled "Lift Up Your Hearts," as well as broadcasting a number of church services at other times of the day. The important thing is that nobody at the time thought this was odd. But fifty years later it is more or less unimaginable.

Not Such a Glorious Victory

The disillusion of the First World War has by now been reinforced by the double disillusion of the Second. In Britain a supposedly glorious victory was followed by two astonishing experiences. The first was a severe economic crisis, made worse by an exceptionally cold winter and appalling pollution — a time of lethal smogs, of frozen pipes and frozen railways, of profound shortages and rationing far more restrictive than it had been during wartime, when supply convoys were being torpedoed by German submarines. Bread had never been rationed in the war. Now it was.

This dismal period made talk of victory seem especially hollow in a country that was still damaged and exhausted by six years of total war. It brought home to those who had not yet understood it the great decline of the country as an economic and political power. The church, associated with discredited authority and supplanted by an increasingly social (as opposed to individual) conscience and social gospel, went into accelerated decline as the pre-war generations of habitual worshipers slowly died away. At around this time, the great missions of Billy Graham to Britain laid the foundations of a new evangelism that has in recent years become a major force in the English church. And the Roman Catholic Church, with its comparatively uncompromising position, seduced many thoughtful English Christians from the increasingly relativistic and agnostic established Church of England. But that established church itself lost authority and, though still present in every corner of England, spoke to and for fewer and fewer people.

It was the 1940s revolutionary period of nationalization, rationing, and growing state power that gave George Orwell the imaginative background for *1984*, his novel about a perpetual socialist future of oppression, regimentation, and shortage. It was coupled with one of the most thorough-going attempts to introduce a socialist state ever attempted in a free country with the rule of law and an elected Parliament. The Labour government elected in 1945, with a huge Parliamentary majority, had many of the characteristics of a revolution, nationalizing private property and centralizing state power, greatly increasing the direct role of government in the national life in a way never before attempted in peacetime (though familiar from the recent war).

Many of that government's measures were popular, not least

the creation of a National Health Service, which made most doctors employees of the state but gave the poor guaranteed free medical treatment. Many of these changes had their roots in English and Scottish radicalism, not in Marxism or Communism, and were inspired by Christian sentiments. The wartime Archbishop of Canterbury, William Temple, had considered himself a Christian Socialist, and much of the Church of England believed that the 1945 Labour government was enacting Christian legislation and turning the country into an ideal Christian society. One effect of this was that the church relinquished control of many of its secondary schools to the state (a mistake the Roman Catholics did not make), in return for the promise of a daily act of Christian worship in all schools — a promise that would be extensively broken within a few decades.

A commitment to social welfare at home and liberal anticolonialism abroad became, in many cases, an acceptable substitute for Christian faith. It is very much so today.

Britain began a long and rather strange era in which it was simultaneously conservative and socialist. Many of its institutions, customs, and traditions were conservative in character, but its government was egalitarian and radical. The conservative elements in the country were strengthened artificially by the outbreak of the Cold War, which identified the more extreme forms of socialism with the national enemy in Moscow. Thus the political conflict between growing secular egalitarianism and the remaining fortresses of Christian conservatism was left unresolved for decades. During this time, the weakness of Christianity among the people and in the schools grew, and cultural revolution of all kinds (described in my 1999 book, *The Abolition of Britain*) continued at all levels.

During the 1960s Christianity was slowly, by gradual degrees, driven into the margins even when religious matters were under discussion. A new generation of teachers, many of them not themselves Christian in any serious way, did not wish to obey the law requiring a daily act of Christian worship in state schools. A revolutionary reorganization of these schools in the 1960s and 1970s, combined with an official decision to widen the recruitment of teachers, coincided with the cultural revolution of the same period. At around the same time, Britain began to absorb (or in many cases fail to absorb) large numbers of migrants from the Indian subcontinent who were not Christian.

On the grounds of good manners, many teachers and local government authorities felt unable to continue to behave as if Christianity were the national religion. It is difficult to tell whether this was motivated in all or most cases by a kindly tactfulness, an attempt at tolerance, or a disguised desire to weaken Christianity, which found multiculturalism a convenient excuse. This led over time to absurd paradoxes such as the existence in some parts of England of "Church of England" primary schools whose pupils are almost exclusively Muslim, thanks to the transformation of those areas by migrant populations. A belief in multiculturalism, promoted by those who disliked the Christian, patriotic monoculture of the country, became common among educationalists and among teachers themselves.

The very idea that Christianity could and should be taught as a belief that the teacher and pupils both shared became increasingly hard to sustain. If it was taught at all, Christianity was explained as something that other people might believe, but that listeners were not expected to embrace themselves. The headquarters of the BBC, the national broadcasting service, is dedicated to Almighty God and adorned with a scriptural exhortation to pursue "whatsoever things are lovely, whatsoever things are true and of good report" (quaecunque pulchra sunt et sincera, quaecunque bonae famae). Yet in recent years BBC announcers began to say of Easter not that it celebrated the Resurrection of Christ but that on this day "Christians celebrate their belief in the resurrection of Christ," or similar neutral formulations.

Had Britain not until recently been a specifically Christian country, these changes would not be so striking. The transition from official Christianity to official religious neutrality has been cautious and gradual and, as such things often are, noticed only by the more committed. It remains incomplete, but the process is clearly visible to the observant. On the main radio channel, a daily Christian service is transmitted but only on the little-used Long-Wave frequency. The confident evangelism of "Lift Up Your Hearts" has been supplanted by a "Thought for the Day," in which Sikhs, Muslims, and Hindus — and the occasional Christian — communicate vapid thoughts on general subjects. The singing of an Easter hymn on the morning of Easter Day appears to have been quietly discontinued. There are religious programs, but often these take the form of a neutral or hostile discussion of religious current affairs, featuring long items about Roman Catholic priests abusing children or Anglican arguments about homosexuality. Alternatively, they show gatherings of elderly people singing hymns. Recently the corporation appointed a Muslim as its head of religious broadcasting.

These things have happened, not because of the rage against

religion in Britain (though such a rage is increasingly common among the intelligentsia for reasons I shall come to), but because the British establishment has ceased to be Christian and has inherited a society with Christian forms and traditions. It does not know what to do with them or how to replace them. Into this confusion and emptiness the new militant secularists now seek to bring an aggressive atheism.

PART 2

ADDRESSING THE THREE FAILED ARGUMENTS OF ATHEISM

CHAPTER 9

"Are Conflicts Fought in the Name of Religion Conflicts about Religion?"

"Why do the heathen so furiously rage together:
and why do the people imagine a vain thing?"

(THE 2ND PSALM)

Among the favorite arguments of the irreligious — one that they almost invariably advance in the opening offensive of their attacks on faith — is this: that conflicts fought in the name of religion are necessarily conflicts about religion. By saying this, the irreligious hope to establish that religion is of itself a cause of conflict. This is a crude factual misunderstanding. Some conflicts fought in the name of religion are specifically religious. Many others are not, or cannot be so simply classified. The only general lesson that can be drawn from these differing wars is that man is inclined to make war on man when he thinks it will gain him power or wealth or land. Atheistic polemicists would reject the crudity and falsity of this argument in seconds if they met it anywhere else. In fact, they tend to apply it only in selective cases, because atheists are most often supporters of the political left, and some wars that *are* caused by religion are sustained by factions and groups with whom the left sympathizes. Consider a few examples.

Conflicts between European Christians

The Thirty Years War (1618 – 48), when much of Europe tore itself to pieces in a conflict between Roman Catholicism and the Reformed Faith, might reasonably be described as a War of Religion. So might the English Civil War, in which radical Calvinists sought to overthrow monarchist Episcopalians, even though both regarded themselves as Protestants. Quarrels about the nature and origin of authority are bound to be religious, but I do not know of any other modern war in which one side's cavalry sang Psalms as they charged, while the other side's troops took Holy Communion as they prepared for battle. These are clearly conflicts about religion.

By contrast, it is perfectly obvious (for instance) that the recent conflict in Northern Ireland, described as being between Protestants and Catholics, was not about the Real Presence of Christ or the validity of the Feast of Corpus Christi or even the authority of the Bishop of Rome. It was a classic tribal war, over the ownership and control of territory, in which the much-decayed faiths of the people involved served as both badge and shorthand for a battle that disgusted the most faithful and enthused the least religious. The processions and funerals of each side were dominated by secular symbols — black berets and combat fatigues — not by holy images or the godly singing of mighty psalms.

Conflicts between Christians, Muslims, and Jews in the Middle East

The same could perhaps be said of the war between Christian and Muslim in Lebanon, where both sides trample on their own scriptures in the cruelty they inflict on each other, yet it is also the case that here Sunni and Shia Muslims overcome deep religious differences for a shared political objective. This would tend to suggest that they are united more by a political distaste for their common enemy than by religious feeling.

But what of the unending confrontation between Israel and the Muslim world? Militant secularists tend to downplay the religious element of this battle, even though in this case there is little doubt that the real issue is Islam's utter refusal to cede any ground that it has once conquered. The question is not whether Jews may live in the Middle East. They are welcome to do so as heavily taxed, powerless, and humiliated second-class citizens in Muslim states, as laid down by the Pact of Umar, which deals with the treatment of "Peoples of the Book" in Muslim nations and is inaccurately described as "tolerant" by many liberal commentators. The question is whether they can maintain a specifically Jewish state on territory recaptured from Islam, a force that tries never to retreat from what it has once conquered (and that still yearns for the lost lands of Spain).

There are several comparable disputes about lost territory and expulsion — from the displaced Aborigines of Australia to the Germans driven from their ancestral homes in the millions under the Potsdam Agreement in the 1940s and the gigantic and blood-soaked forced migrations of Hindus and Muslims during the India-Pakistan partition of 1947. In that last case, the partition and expulsions were not brought about by a Hindu victory over Islam, but the result of the campaign among Indian Muslims for a state of their own, a sort of Muslim Israel.

None of these sad stories has the same everlasting and insoluble quality as the expulsion of Arabs from Palestine in 1948. None of the German refugees from Poland, the Czech Lands, or East Prussia in 1945 – 47 still dwells in a refugee camp, nor do the many Jews expelled from the Arab and Muslim world after the foundation of Israel; whereas the camps for those Arabs expelled from Israel in 1948 are now much bigger than they were then, and their inhabitants are kept where they are and prevented from improving their living conditions, mainly for propaganda reasons. What is more, while the Muslim impulse against Israel is profoundly religious, Israel is in almost all ways a secular state, founded by irreligious, socialist non-Jewish Jews and actively disliked as blasphemous by many of the most Orthodox Jews. Its easily evaded marriage laws — one of the few religious things about its legal system — are misleadingly cited by critics as evidence that Israel is a theocracy, when it is nothing of the kind.

The strangest thing of all is that the European secular left (with few exceptions) disapproves strongly of Israel and often denounces it inaccurately as religiously intolerant; yet it seldom if ever characterizes the Muslim coalition against Israel as theocratic or reactionary. Why is this? In general, the Western secular left (as did for many years the Soviet Union) has sympathized with the Islamic campaign against Israel since the 1967 Arab-Israeli war turned that country from a surrounded and endangered island of beleaguered territory into a colonial power occupying large amounts of territory inhabited by Arabs. One of the greatest problems for leftists recently converted to neo-conservative support for the war in Iraq and for bombing Iran is that they suddenly find themselves alongside Israel, a country they have despised for decades because they regard it as a survival of the colonial era.

The Left's hostility to Christianity is actually specific, because Christianity is the religion of their own homes and homeland, the form in which they have encountered — and generally disliked and resented — the power of God in their own lives. Islam, for most of the Left's time on earth, has been an exotic and distant creed, never taught to them as a living faith and never likely to be their own or to require their obedience. Therefore the Left can sympathize with it as the enemy of their Christian monoculture and as an anti-colonial and therefore "progressive" force. Some Marxist leftists in Britain have taken this to its logical conclusion and have formed alliances with British Muslims despite the Muslims' highly conservative attitudes toward women and homosexuals. Others prefer to live in a state of unresolved doublethink.

This position is becoming harder and harder to maintain as Islam grows in power and reach, and as it becomes a major religious force in many nations of Europe, where so many "progressives" live. The growing dalliance of radicals with anti-Islamic neo-conservatism is one consequence. But it is an awkward fit, despite the utopian atheism that is common among such neo-conservatives. As much as they dislike Islam's role as the intolerant censor of novels and cartoonists, as the enemy of feminism, and as a harsh voice of sexual conservatism, the western liberal Left have spent too long as Islam's ally against Israel, or as defenders of mass immigration by Muslims into European countries, to be wholly convincing on this point. Meanwhile, neo-conservatism's overheated suspicion of Islam contrasts quite ludicrously with its dogmatic support for mass immigration, the so-called "free movement of labor," and its relaxed view of multiculturalism. If there is a Muslim threat in the Western world, it comes much more from the fast-expanding Islamic populations there than from terrorism. The neo-conservative position is only sustainable because neo-conservatism's main base is in the USA, where most immigration is Latin American and multiculturalism means speaking Spanish. If Mexicans were Muslims and spoke Arabic or Urdu, things would be very different.

Then there is Afghanistan, where the nominally Christian West, having once mobilized warrior Islam against the Soviet Union (which was the ally of the Arabs in their war against Israel), now fights a furious war against warrior Islam. Islam in its turn has repaid past American help with terrorist attacks on New York and Washington, D.C. Amusingly, it was the USSR that once claimed to be liberating the women of Afghanistan from the tyranny of Islam, a task it had successfully achieved in its own Central Asian empire. Now it is the "West," which tried so hard to drive the USSR out of Afghanistan, that says its troops must remain there ... to protect Afghan women from the tyranny of Islam. Is this a war caused by religion, or by human folly?

Conflicts between Christians and Muslims in the Balkans

Interestingly, in news reports on the recent (1991 – 95) conflict in Yugoslavia — which might have been described as between

Christian and Muslim — the terms Serb, Croat, and Bosnian were generally used to describe the combatants, rather than Orthodox, Catholic, and Muslim. Most Western commentators were consistently more sympathetic to the Bosnians than to other groups, but not because they were Muslims. It was mainly because they idealized Bosnia's allegedly multi-ethnic state as a model for the borderless globalism that they hope to see introduced everywhere in their imagined utopia.

Yet, in other times this was not so. Balkan Muslims were the undoubted villains in the days of the Bulgarian Horrors, which stirred the liberal-minded people of Britain against the Turks in the nineteenth century. Their part in the twentieth-century race wars was not honorable either. When the German SS recruited a division from among Bosnian Muslims, it was their Islamic hostility to Jews that appealed most of all to the National Socialists. At that time the Serbs, now the official villains of the conflict, were the principal allies of the "West" on the Balkan Peninsula.

Those who blame religion for wars tend to do so only when it suits them to do so, and without paying much attention to the details. In this debate, they generally mean "Christianity" when they say religion. Christianity is their actual target. They may now denounce Islam as fervently as they wish and flaunt their courage in doing so, but the secular left's true relationship with Islam is equivocal, especially over the issue of Israel and over multiculturalism in previously Christian states. And Islam is entirely uncowed and undented by the New Atheism or by neo-conservatism. It is, in general, proof against any secular weapon and is less impressed than many think by Western wealth, military power, or political liberty. Islam is, in fact, likely to be the main long-term beneficiary of the collapse of Christianity in Europe, at least, where Islam is already a sizeable minority faith through immigration and population growth. Islam will be well placed to benefit from any future revival of religious feeling in countries where Christianity is rapidly losing both its following and its position.

The current intellectual assault on God in Europe and North America is in fact a specific attack on Christianity — the faith that stubbornly persists in the morality, laws, and government of the major Western countries. Despite the self-conscious militancy of some of the anti-theists against Islam, they rarely encounter organized Islam in their own countries, are sensibly wary of challenging Islam on its own ground, and seldom debate with Muslim spokesmen (who are not interested in discussing an issue they believe to be closed). Their hostility to Islam as a "threat to our way of life" is a result of their late realization that it might, if it became powerful, menace the license in sexual and other matters that their cause has won, thanks to the weakness of Christianity in its former domains. The God they fight is the Christian God, because he is their own God, as I explain above. But what is it that they have against the Christian God?

God is the leftists' chief rival. Christian belief, by subjecting all men to divine authority and by asserting in the words "My kingdom is not of this world" that the ideal society does not exist in this life, is the most coherent and potent obstacle to secular utopianism. Christ's reproof of Judas — "the poor always ye have with you" — when Judas complains that precious ointment could have been sold to feed the poor rather than applied to Jesus' feet (see John 12:1 – 8 KJV), is also a stumbling-block and an annoyance to world reformers. By putting such socialistic thoughts in the mouth of the despised traitor-to-be Judas, and by stating so baldly the truth known to all conservatives that poverty cannot be eradicated, the Bible angers and frustrates those who believe that the pursuit of a perfect society justifies the quest for absolute power.

The concepts of sin, of conscience, of eternal life, and of divine justice under an unalterable law are the ultimate defense against the utopian's belief that ends justify means and that morality is relative. These concepts are safeguards against the worship of human power. Now, that conflict is made sharper still by the alliance between political utopianism and the new cult of the unrestrained self, unleashed into the Western world by Sigmund Freud and Wilhelm Reich, by Alfred Kinsey and Herbert Marcuse, promoted by the self-pitying anthems of rock music, and encouraged by the enormous power of "progressive" education in which so many cultural revolutionaries work. The last of these — by refusing to teach the previously accepted canon of literature, history, and philosophy, by attempting to turn Christianity into a museum-piece, and by abandoning the concept of authority — has left advanced societies entirely disarmed against intellectual assaults they could once have repulsed with ease. These influences were the real driving force of the 1960s social, sexual, and moral revolution that now seeks to destroy the last remaining restraints on its victory.

There is a general belief in the West that Marxist revolution came to a bitter and conclusive end with the fall of the Soviet Union and the European Communist regimes in 1989 – 91. On the contrary, the New Left were released from painful bonds by this collapse. No longer were they burdened with the failure of the Soviet experiment, which could always be used to argue against them. They were free at last from the identification of radical politics with the Kremlin enemy, which kept them out of political power in the Western democracies.

While they were relieved by the collapse of the decrepit Soviet Union, many radicals retain a regard for the impulses that began it. We now view the 1917 Russian Revolution as an unmitigated failure, soaked in blood and buried in infamy. But a surprising number of modern liberal leftists retain a sentimental belief in its initial goodness and would in its early years have identified with it. They do not believe its failure was inevitable or a result of its nature, and in many cases they wish it had succeeded.

The existence of Trotskyism as a strong force among Western intellectuals in the 1960s and 1970s, especially in Europe, is interesting evidence of this, since Trotskyism is essentially a deluded pretence that the Bolshevik Revolution might have succeeded in other hands than Stalin's. Many of those who took essentially Trotskyist positions in those years went on to become influential in politics, the academy, journalism, the law, and the arts in the years that followed. It is therefore important to recognize two things — that the Russian Revolution was an earlier version of the modern revolt against God; and that today's anti-Christian revolutionaries would very much prefer to disown the apostolic succession that leads from Lenin and Stalin to them, preferring to identify with the slain heretic and martyr of Stalin, Leon Trotsky. This view is only sustainable because Trotsky, a bloodthirsty enthusiast for repression in his short years of power, was a failure who was never able to demonstrate in practice that he was at least as evil as Stalin. Thanks to this belief, Stalin can be treated as if he were an aberration, and any suggestion that his regime's savagery was connected with its atheism must be vigorously denied. Serious historians of the Russian Revolution (notably Richard Pipes) and biographers of Trotsky (notably Robert Service) make nonsense of the claim that Trotsky in power would have been preferable to or greatly different from Stalin.

More importantly for this debate, the record shows that an actual systematic hatred for Christianity was central to the Soviet regime, flowing directly from its materialist philosophy and pursued at some cost and with some difficulty (as I shall shortly show). But first, a short diversion is necessary to deal with the problem of National Socialist Germany. In that country, the Christian churches largely, but not entirely, failed in their duty of opposition. Yet an essentially secular and anti-Christian regime, more pagan than atheist, was preparing their destruction in any case. The undoubted National Socialist loathing of Christianity tells us more about that faith than do the actions of the leaders of the churches.

The Undeniable Link between Atheism and Anti-Theist Regimes

I am (as I explain at greater length in a later chapter) baffled and frustrated by the strange insistence of my anti-theist brother that the cruelty of Communist anti-theist regimes does not reflect badly on his case and on his cause. It unquestionably does. Soviet Communism is organically linked to atheism, materialist rationalism, and most of the other causes the New Atheists support. It used the same language, treasured the same hopes, and appealed to the same constituency as atheism does today. When its crimes were still unknown, or concealed, it attracted the support of the liberal intelligentsia who were then, and are even more now, opposed to religion.

My brother and his allies, who can now confidently classify the Soviet regime as "Stalinist" and so evade any responsibility for it, must ask themselves with ruthless honesty what they would have thought and said about it at the time, before such escape routes were open. They must ask themselves which questionable causes and regimes they have made excuses for in this age, and consider the possibility that utopianism is dangerous precisely because its supporters are so convinced that they are themselves good.

Even after its evils became widely known, the same liberal intelligentsia continued in many cases to sympathize with the USSR and defend it against conservative and Christian critics. Soviet power was — as it was intended to be — the opposite of faith in God. It was faith in the greatness of humanity and in the perfectibility of human society. The atheists cannot honestly disown it, and it is because they know this in their hearts that they panic and babble when confronted with the problem. Nothing else can explain the absurd denials they issue.

Christianity and the Third Reich

But what of the USSR's loathly opposite, the Hitlerian Third Reich? I am not going to argue here that the Nazi state was an atheist state, because I do not believe the matter is so simple, and I do not wish to rely on easy arguments, caricature my opponents, or smear them by association. The relation between National Socialism and the churches, in Hitler's twelve years in power, was often awkward but not always hostile. To begin with, the Nazis needed at least the neutrality of the Christian middle classes. Had they had time, they would have come into ever-greater conflict with believers. Clearly, the Hitler Youth and the general propaganda of National Socialism were increasing rivals to family and church — meetings of Nazi youth deliberately timed to clash with church services and festivals, messages of sexual promiscuity and rebellion against parental authority contrary to Christian teaching. In this, the youth movements of Nazi Germany and Communist Russia were startlingly similar. Any ideological or revolutionary state must alienate the young from their pre-revolutionary parents if it hopes to survive into future generations. But in Germany it never lasted long enough to demonstrate this fully. And while it gathered its power, the Christian religion did not fight as fiercely or as bravely as it ought to have done.

The behavior of the churches toward National Socialism was variable, as the behavior of men and women always is when they are frightened or confused. There were total fawning, surrenders, and revolting attempts to create a Nazified Christianity in which the Jewish heritage of the faith was expunged and denied. There were acts of great courage by Christians of all faiths. There were rather more moments of shameful compromise and also of miserable persecution. What is the significance of this? Does it reveal that Christianity as a religion sympathized with the National Socilalists? Hardly. Does it reveal that Christians often failed in their duty? Undoubtedly. What is missing is some sort of organic connection linking the Nazis with Christianity, or vice versa. I have no doubt that those on the political and cultural left seek such a connection precisely because they wish to defend themselves against their own concern that there is an organic connection between their cause and that of Stalinist Communism, the connection which above all they wish to deny.

CHAPTER 10

"Is it Possible to Determine What Is Right and What Is Wrong without God?"

"I will run the way of thy commandments
when thou hast set my heart at liberty."

(THE 119TH PSALM)

The second atheist problem is the unbelievers' assertion that it is possible to determine what is right and what is wrong without God. They have a fundamental inability to concede that to be effectively absolute, a moral code needs to be beyond human power to alter. On this misunderstanding is based my brother Christopher's supposed conundrum about whether there is any good deed that could be done only by a religious person and not done by a Godless one. Like all such questions, this contains another question — what is good, and who is to decide what is good?

Left to themselves, human beings can in a matter of minutes justify the incineration of populated cities, the mass deportation — accompanied by slaughter, disease, and starvation — of inconvenient people, and the mass murder of the unborn. I have heard people who believe themselves to be good defend all these things and convince themselves as well as others. Quite often the same people will condemn similar actions committed by different countries, often with great vigor.

I have done both of these things myself. The Second World War, in which the good side committed dreadful crimes and the bad side worse ones, is a constant source of such confusion. And, as it is so often used as a model for new interventionist wars, it continues to influence the actions and fates of millions. Anyone who speaks the unpleasant truth about that war, and especially about the bombing of civilians, is met to this day with rage and resentment, just as is anyone who draws attention to the unpleasant truth about abortion (the one act of violence that British television refuses to show).

It is plain even from these few recent examples that for a moral code to be effective, the code must be attributed to, and vested in, a non-human source. It must be beyond the power of humanity to change it to suit itself. If that non-human source can be shown to be false, then the moral code that it endorses cannot be absolute. It will become a matter of choice, or have to be kept in place by the threat of force, or a mixture of both, like any other code of human invention.

In their attempt to argue that effective and binding codes can be developed without a deity, atheists often mistake inferior codes of "common decency" for absolute moral systems. The Golden Rule, or doing as you would be done by, is such a code. But the fact that people can arrive at the Golden Rule without religion does not mean that they can arrive at the Christian moral code without religion. Christianity requires much more and, above all, does not expect to see charity returned. To "love thy neighbor as thyself" is a far greater and more complicated obligation, requiring a positive effort to seek the good of others, often in secret, sometimes at great cost, and always without reward. Its most powerful expression is summed up in the words "Greater love hath no man than this, that a man lay down his life for his friends" (John 15:13 KJV). The huge differences that can be observed between Christian societies and all others, even in the twilit afterglow of Christianity, originate in this specific injunction.

It is striking that in his dismissal of a need for absolute theistic morality, my brother Christopher states that "the order to 'love thy neighbour *as thyself*' is too extreme and too strenuous to be obeyed"[1] Humans, he says, "are not so constituted as to care for others as much as themselves." This is demonstrably untrue and can be shown to be untrue — first, through the unshakeable devotion of mothers to their children; through thousands of examples of doctors and nurses risking (and undergoing) infection and death in the course of caring for others; in the uncounted cases of husbands caring for sick, incontinent, and demented wives (and vice versa) at their lives' ends; through the heartrending deeds of courage on the battlefield, of men actually laying down their lives for others. We all know that these things happen. If we are honest, they make us uncomfortable because we are not sure that we could do such things, though we know them to be right and admirable.

In a society where the absolute code has been jettisoned and we have all become adept at making excuses for shirking such duties, selflessness of this kind will become less common, nursing less dedicated, wives more inclined to leave their babbling husbands in care homes to be looked after impersonally by

1. *God Is Not Great* (New York: Twelve, 2007), 213.

paid strangers and perhaps encouraged gently down the slope of death, and soldiers readier to save themselves while their comrades lie in pain within reach of the enemy. And there will always be a worldly relativist on hand (as there already is at every marriage break-up and every abortion clinic and increasingly by the bedside of the old and sick) to say that this is only sensible, to urge that we do the easy thing, and to say that it is right to do so.

Christianity is without doubt difficult and taxing, and all of us fail to emulate the perfection of Christ himself. But we are far better for trying than for not trying, and we know that there is forgiveness available for honest failure. My brother's suggestion that we are urged to be superhuman "on pain of death and torture" reveals a misunderstanding both of the nature of the commandments and of the extent of forgiveness. There is also some excuse-making involved. The difficult is being described as superhuman. Yes, there is fear in the Christian constitution, as there must be in any system of law and justice. I should be dismayed if deliberate, unrepentant wickedness did not lead to retribution of some kind. But there is far more love offered for those who honestly attempt to follow the law, and unbounded forgiveness for all who seek it — even those who have most vigorously defamed the faith and then embrace it just before the darkness falls. And that is why, while it is perfectly possible for convinced atheists to do absolutely good deeds at great cost to themselves — not least because God so very much wishes them to — it is rather more likely that believing Christians will do such things. And when it comes to the millions of small and tedious good deeds that are needed for a society to function with charity, honesty, and kindness, a shortage of believing Christians will lead to that society's decay.

We can live at a low level of cooperation by mutual consideration. But as soon as we move beyond subsistence and the smallest units, problems arise that cannot be resolved by mutual decency. Some people grow richer, some are stronger, some acquire weapons. Power comes into being at a very early stage in human society. So do greed, competition for scarce resources, and wars with other groups. Mutual benefit ceases to offer any kind of guide to behavior. Who is to say, in a city ruled by a single powerful and ruthless family from an impregnable fortress, that the strongest man is not also always right? In fact, the Godless principle that the strongest is always right has been openly declared as recently as the twentieth century in Mussolini's Italy and operated in practice in Hitler's Germany, Stalin's Soviet Union, and many other states.

In wars, men are repeatedly asked to undertake acts of selfless courage that they will not themselves survive. Men are expected to be responsible for the women who bear their children, for as long as they live. Women in return are expected to be faithful to those men. For economies to develop, men must be trusted to guard valuables that are not their own. Again and again, for civilization to exist and advance, human creatures are required to do things that they would not do "naturally" as mammals. Marriage is unnatural. Building for the future is unnatural. The practice of medicine is unnatural. The deferment of immediate gratification for a greater reward is unnatural. Charity is unnatural. Education is unnatural. Literacy is unnatural, as is the passing on of lore and history from one generation to another. The Beaver may be able to build a dam, but it has always been the same dam, and it will always be the same dam. Only mankind can advance from making huts out of branches to building the Parthenon (and only mankind can fall back from the Parthenon to shacks and caves).

Mankind's immense artistic talent is visible in the paintings on the walls of the Cro-Magnon caves of Lascaux. The sublime heights to which that talent can rise in the midst of a great Christian civilization can be seen in the works of the Italian and Flemish masters. The debasement of that talent by the rejection of the very springs and origin of civilization can likewise be seen in much of the work of modern artists.

Christian societies as a whole are "unnatural," requiring a host of actions that cannot be based on self-interest, however enlightened, or even on mutual obligation. Meanwhile, the more civilized a society is, the more power is available within it. Power cannot be destroyed, only divided and distributed. It may shatter into an anarchic war of all against all. Or it may solidify into a tyranny. Or it may be resolved into a free society governed by universally acknowledged laws. But on what basis can this be done? What agency can be used to place law above force? A law that does not stand above brute force and have some sort of power that can overcome brute force will not survive for long. How are inconvenient obligations, those of the banker and the messenger and the merchant, to be made binding? How are the young to be made to accept the authority of parents and teachers, once they are physically strong enough to ignore them, but too inexperienced in life to know the value of peace and learning?

The answer, from a very early stage, is that such contracts were made binding by solemn promises sworn in the name of Almighty God and, as Abraham Lincoln used to say of his Presidential Oath, "registered in heaven." These oaths called into every contract an external power — one whose awful vengeance no man could escape if he defied it, and which he would be utterly ashamed to break. As Sir Thomas More explains in Robert Bolt's play *A Man for All Seasons*, when a man swears an oath, "He's holding his own self in his own hands. Like water. And if he opens his fingers *then* — he needn't hope to find himself again."

In their utter reverence for oaths, men of More's era were in my view as superior to us as the builders of Chartres Cathedral were to the builders of shopping malls. Our ancestors' undisturbed faith gave them a far closer, healthier relation to the truth — and so to beauty — than we have. Without a belief in God and the soul, where is the oath? Without the oath, where is the obligation or the pressure to fulfill it? Where is the law that even kings must obey? Where is Magna Carta, Habeas Corpus, or the Bill of Rights, all of which arose out of attempts to rule by lawless tyranny? Where is the lifelong fidelity of husband and wife? Where is the safety of the innocent child growing in the womb? Where, in the end, is the safety of any of us from those currently bigger and stronger than we are?

And how striking it is that such oaths were used to make us better, not worse, and that the higher power, the magnetic north of moral truth, found an invariable answer in the urgings of conscience. These things are far higher than the mutuality and "human solidarity" on which atheists must rely for morality — because they specifically deny the existence of any other origin for it.

This is not, alas, an argument for or against the existence

of God, though it might just be an argument for the existence of good, with humankind left wondering how to discover what is good and what good is. It simply states the price that may sooner or later have to be paid for presuming that God does not exist and then removing him from human affairs.

It also sets out the important benefit that can be obtained by placing God at the heart of a society. I should have thought that those who are serious about their unbelief would be relieved by this logic and glad to concede it. If they know, or are reasonably certain, that there is no ultimate authority and no judgment issuing from some unalterable law, they are instantly quite extraordinarily free. But this freedom is as available to monsters and power-seekers as it is to advanced intellectuals dwelling in comfortable suburbs. And that leads to the state of affairs correctly summed up by the German philosopher Martin Heidegger, who in 1933 proclaimed from among the lovely towers and groves of the university at Freiburg-im-Breisgau that "The Führer, and he alone, is the present and future law of Germany." Alas, he was absolutely right, and Adolf Hitler himself had to be destroyed before that law could be canceled.

If atheists or anti-theists have the good fortune to live in a society still governed by religious belief, or even its afterglow, they may feel free from absolute moral bonds, while those around them are not. This is a tremendous liberation for anyone who is even slightly selfish. And what clever person is not imaginatively and cunningly selfish?

Oddly enough, very few atheists are as delighted by this prospect as they ought to be. At least they are not delighted openly or in public. Could this be because they really do not grasp this astonishingly simple point, based as it is on their own insistence that the most plausible external source of law and morality does not exist? Why create such a difficulty for themselves at all? Might it be because they fear that, by admitting their delight at the non-existence of good and evil, they are revealing something of their motives for their belief? Could it be that the last thing on earth they wish to acknowledge is that they *have* motives for their belief, since by doing so they would open up their flanks to attack?

One interesting answer to this question of "why do atheists want there to be no God?" comes from Thomas Nagel, professor of philosophy and law at New York University and no friend of religion. In his book *The Last Word*, Nagel writes,[2]

> Even without God, the idea of a natural sympathy between the deepest truths of nature and the deepest layers of the human mind, which can be exploited to allow gradual development of a true and truer conception of reality, makes us more *at home* in the universe than is secularly comfortable. The thought that the relation between the mind and the world is something fundamental makes many people in this day and age nervous.

Nagel then says:

> I believe this is one manifestation of a fear of religion which has large and often pernicious consequences for modern intellectual life.
>
> In speaking of the fear of religion, I don't mean to refer to the entirely reasonable hostility toward certain established

---

2. New York: Oxford University Press, 2001.

religions and religious institutions, in virtue of their objectionable moral doctrines, social policies and political influence. Nor am I referring to the association of many religious beliefs with superstition and the acceptance of evident empirical falsehoods. I am talking about something much deeper — namely, the fear of religion itself. I speak from experience, being strongly subject to this fear myself: I want atheism to be true and am made uneasy by the fact that some of the most intelligent and well-informed people I know are religious believers. It isn't just that I don't believe in God and, naturally, hope that I'm right in my belief. It's that I hope there is no God! I don't want there to be a God; I don't want the universe to be like that.

According to Professor Nagel, who has no ulterior motive for saying so, this fear has produced some poor science among his fellow unbelievers:

My guess is that this cosmic authority problem is not a rare condition and that it is responsible for much of the scientism and reductionism of our time. One of the tendencies it supports is the ludicrous overuse of evolutionary biology to explain everything about life, including everything about the human mind.

And he even notes in an important aside a problem that many Christians, who are also physicists, have observed:

There might still be thought to be a religious threat in the existence of the laws of physics themselves, and indeed the existence of anything at all—but it seems to be less alarming to most atheists.

This is the sort of argument I personally long to hear from atheists—one that recognizes the possible attractions to the intelligent mind of the religious explanation rather than denouncing all religious belief as stupid. Nagel, disappointingly, has little to say about the precise source of the fear he describes. Why would anyone fear the idea of God? I can think of many reasons, myself, usually concerned with the annoying and lingering possibility of divine punishment for unexpiated wrongdoing. But we must not mention this in the twenty-first century. In a footnote, Nagel says he

won't attempt to speculate about the Oedipal and other sources of either this desire or its opposite. (About the latter there has already been considerable speculation—Freud's *The Future of an Illusion*, for example.) I am curious, however, whether there is anyone who is genuinely indifferent as to whether there is a God—anyone who, whatever his actual belief about the matter, doesn't particularly *want* either one of the answers to be correct (though of course he might want to *know* which answer was correct).

I would counter, as a believer, that I most definitely have motives for my belief. I believe in God and the Christian religion at least partly because it suits me to do so. I prefer to believe that I live in an ordered universe with a purpose that I can at least partly discover. I derive my ideas of what is absolutely true and what is absolutely right from this source. I need these ideas many times each day. How else can I function as a parent, as a citizen, as a reporter? I should be desolated if it could ever be proved that theism is false. But I am human, fallen and flawed, so I am slippery about this faith (which has a reasonably good effect on me when I try hard to follow it, but can be a great nuisance to me when I wish to follow the devices and desires of my own heart).

From time to time I also try to wriggle out of the laws to which I have sworn obedience. I then reject parts of the teaching of my faith, those parts that condemn what I want to think or say or do. I can usually find clever and ingenious arguments for doing this. I invariably do so because it suits me personally. In this, I am doing exactly what the atheist does, only not to the same extent, because I do not actively wish for disorder and meaninglessness, and I recognize that if I pull down the pillars of the moral universe, I too will be crushed when the roof falls. So I follow my failure with regret and hope for forgiveness (yet again). This is an argument for the belief that humanity is imperfect and fallen, not a condemnation of faith or of God. And in all my experience of life, I have seldom seen a more powerful argument for the fallen nature of man, and his inability to achieve perfection, than those countries in which man set himself up to replace God with the state.

CHAPTER 11

"Are Atheist States Not Actually Atheist?"

"Take heed, ye unwise among the people:
O ye fools, when will ye understand?"

(THE 94TH PSALM)

Let us examine the strange problem of the Atheist states, which a ruthlessly honest Godless person must surely admit as a difficulty. After all, intelligent Christians must — if they are candid — accept that faith has often led to cruel violence and intolerant persecution. They may say, as I would, that this was because humans often misunderstand or misuse the teachings of the religions they follow. This is not because they are religious, but because Man is not great.

Atheists, in return, ought equally to concede that Godless regimes and movements have given birth to terrible persecutions and massacres. They do not do so, in my view, because in these cases the slaughter is not the result of a misunderstanding or excessive zeal. Utopia can only ever be approached across a sea of blood. This is a far greater problem for the atheist than it is for the Christian, because the atheist uses this argument to try to demonstrate that religion specifically makes things worse than they otherwise would be. On the contrary, it demonstrates that our ability to be savage to our own kind cannot be wholly prevented by religion. More important still, Atheist states have a consistent tendency to commit mass murders in the name of the greater good.

It is difficult to claim that Christianity has learned nothing from its past cruelty or that such cruelty is written in its laws or prescribed by its beliefs. When did Christians last burn, strangle, or imprison each other for alleged errors of faith? By contrast, those who reject God's absolute authority, preferring their own, are far more ready to persecute than Christians have been and have grown more included to do so over time. Each revolutionary generation reliably repeats the savagery. The Bolsheviks knew all about the French revolutionary terror, but that did not stop them having their own. The Chinese Communists knew all about Stalin's intentional famine and five-year-plans, but they repeated the barbarity with the Great Leap Forward. The Khmer Rouge were not ignorant of their revolutionary forerunners, yet they repeated the evil worse than before. The supposedly enlightened revolution of Fidel Castro resorted swiftly to torture and arbitrary imprisonment and to the lawless purging and murder even of Castro's old comrades such as Huber Matos. By comparison, where now do we see Christian churches or factions persecuting each other as they did in the Reformation or Counter-Reformation? Nowhere. The delusion of revolutionary progress, and the ruthlessness it justifies, survives any amount of experience. This suggests that terror and slaughter are inherent in utopian materialist revolutionary movements. There will be another of these episodes along soon. What, then, do we gain by rejecting God and worshiping ourselves instead?

But atheists cannot bear to look their faith's faults full in the face. They cannot even admit that their dogmatic insistence that there is no God is in fact a faith, though they cannot possibly know if they are right. Their belief, apparently, is not even a belief. And so the escape clauses come thick and fast. If atheism in practice appears at any point to have had bad consequences, that is because it took on the character of religion. So this murder, that massacre, that purge just do not count. If religious people do good things with good consequences, that is because they are really atheists without knowing it.

We are told by my brother, for example, that Joseph Stalin's Soviet Union was in fact a religious state. In the mouth of any other person, serving a cause other than the comfortable West's rejection of self-restraint and divine law, such thin, self-serving stuff would produce scorn and mockery from the anti-religion advocates. As I show in a later chapter, the specifically anti-religious (and more specifically, anti-Christian) character of the Soviet system under Stalin makes such a claim nonsensical. To say that Stalin used many of the outward forms of religion is perfectly reasonable and true. But to claim that the outward forms are more important than the inward character is plainly false. It is precisely the inward character — submission to an earthly authority instead of an eternal authority — that makes all the difference.

The Humanist Cult in Stalin's Russia and Kim Il Sung's North Korea

Stalin's system resembled religion in one important way. Stalin, who had been schooled in a seminary, wished to be worshiped —

despite the fact that he was a man and not God. Kim Il Sung (brought up as a Protestant and an accomplished church organist) sought the same goal. Both men understood very well the power of religion over the human mind. Both deliberately chose not to use religion to sustain their regimes, as the Russian tsars had sought to do; they chose a far more difficult course. They hated faith in God so much that they instead destroyed it and supplanted it with a humanist cult that vested all power in themselves and that — unlike true religion — was bound to die.

In North Korea this did not involve as much destruction as in Russia, since Christianity was not so well-established there and ancient traditions, rather than a deity, tend to prevail. There is no war on these traditions as such, and especially not on ancestor-worship, since it does not conflict with the regime, but marches merrily alongside it.

By great good fortune I have witnessed, on a beautiful autumn morning, what seemed to be the entire population of Pyongyang streaming out of the city on bicycles and in buses, for the ancient Korean harvest festival of Chuseok, which involves (among other things) eating rice-cakes in the shape of the crescent moon and holding picnics amid the hilltop graves of your forefathers. No attempt was being made to suppress this survival, and in fact the people had worked the previous Sunday, by government order, so as to take the correct day off for the feast, a date governed by the moon rather than by the state. There was no menace in this prehistoric pagan rite to the authority of the Dear and Great Leaders. Why not? Because even if millions of people took part in it, it did not challenge the authority of State, Party, or Leader. No alternative allegiance was required. By contrast, a single secret celebration of Christian Holy Communion, involving three or four people honestly pledging themselves to be ruled by a rival authority, would — if discovered — have been suppressed with all the fury and venom the state could muster.

Stalin and Kim made human idols of themselves because they believed — as utopian idealists always do — in the ultimate goodness of themselves and the unchallengeable rightness of their decisions. There was no higher power, and so there could be no higher law. If people disagreed with them, it was because those people were in some way defective — insane, malignant, or mercenary. The rulers could not tolerate actual religion because they could not tolerate any rival authority or any rival source — or judge — of goodness, rectitude, and justice.

Modern revolutionaries frequently make a point of openly and specifically rejecting the very idea of absolute, unalterable goodness outside time and space. Bela Kun, whose Hungarian Soviet Republic mimicked Lenin's Russian original, proclaimed that none of his acts were either moral or immoral. The only test of his state was whether it benefited the Proletariat. And he was the judge of that. George Lukacs, a Commissar for Culture and Education in Kun's mercifully brief government, is credibly said once to have advised a comrade (Ilona Duczynska): "Communist ethics make it the highest duty to accept the necessity of acting wickedly. This is the greatest sacrifice the revolution asks from us. The conviction of the true Communist is that evil transforms itself into good through the dialectics of historical evolution." The same shifty Lukacs continues to this day to attract admirers among radical intellectuals. It is important to grasp that the Marxist moral worldview has no lower limit and that its most charming, civilized, and tasteful adherents all necessarily share the same lack of scruple — Jesuits with no fear of hellfire.

This sort of belief is not just the thinking of a small-town bully such as Stalin. The charming, witty, well-educated, and still-admired Bolshevik Nikolai Bukharin, in his 1921 book *Theory of Historical Materialism*, viewed ethics as useless, fetishistic survivals of old class standards. He compared the proletariat to a carpenter.

> If the proletariat wishes to attain communism, then it must do such and such, as does the carpenter in building a bench. And whatever is expedient from this point of view, this must be done. "Ethics" transforms itself for the proletariat, step by step, into simple and comprehensible rules of conduct necessary for communism and in point of fact, ceases to be ethics.

This very logic brought about Bukharin's torture and death.

The same might be said of Leon Trotsky, who sneered in *Their Morals and Ours* in 1938:

> Whoever does not care to return to Moses, Christ or Mohammed; whoever is not satisfied with eclectic hodge-podges must acknowledge that morality is a product of social development; that there is nothing invariable about it; that it serves social interests; that these interests are contradictory; that morality more than any other form of ideology has a class character.

Trotsky also — rightly — pointed out that Christians often manipulate their own precepts to suit themselves. But, in the way of Marxists, he could not see that this was a criticism of their humanity, not of their Christianity. If they had stuck to their beliefs, they would have been unequivocally better than any Bolshevik. It was their failure to do so that rightly opened them to his derision. His old foe Stalin, employing the same moral code, thought it served the proletarian cause to have Trotsky murdered in 1940.

Those familiar with Marxist squabbles will know that there is no final court of appeal on such matters. "History," written by the victors, is said to be the judge. This means that those who win are also right, which is and must be the core of all ad-hoc human-based moral codes.

Leaders Who Abuse Piety for Non-Christian Ends

The distinction between such regimes and those that have employed the church as a moral police force is enormous. One replaces God with itself. The other seeks to conscript God into its service and is happy to allow conscience to flourish in large areas of private life, because it is not interested in total power. We might cite the Presidency of George W. Bush, which combined noisy religiosity with ruthlessness, as a modern example of the second type. Something similar could be said about Britain's Prime Minister Anthony Blair, who was ostentatiously pious while conniving with his intelligence services to manufacture pretexts for aggressive war. Such governments are repellent. The conscription of God into unjust wars does grave harm to faith.

But these leaders were — as they found out — limited in their actions by the very Christianity they exploited.

Both Mr. Blair's New Labour Party and George W. Bush's

Republicans were gravely injured by their blasphemous attempt to enlist heaven in aggressive war. Mr. Bush also undoubtedly hurt Christianity in America by allying it to his war and his administration. The ultimate effects of this error on the part of many church leaders may take years to emerge, just as the European churches' support for the First World War took decades to devastate those churches. But among younger people especially, I believe great damage has been done.

No such problems — no limits placed on them by faith — troubled the Soviet Communist authorities when they set out to crush and marginalize Islam in Soviet Central Asia, a few hundred miles north of Iraq. Stalin's atheist conquest of this vast Musim region, confidently immoral and wholly secular, endured for decades. It succeeded in forcibly unveiling and educating women (compulsory mass burnings of headscarves were held in city squares) and driving the Imams of Islam into the farthest corners of their societies. Yet one does not hear the supporters of the "War on Terror" endorsing this action or using it as an example to be followed, even though it was far more successful in weakening Islam than anything they have ever done or ever will do. And why should it not have been? Without God, many more actions are possible than are permitted in a Godly order. Atheism is a license for ruthlessness, and it appeals to the ruthless.

The Dangerous Intolerance of Supposedly Enlightened Atheists

Is this ruthlessness to be directed only against Islam? It seems not. As I will show, some of the arguments of atheists also lead them into a dangerous intolerance of Christian moral opinions and of the Christian education of children, which does not sit well with their self-image as apostles of enlightenment and liberty. Like all foes of liberty, they are all for it except when they are really, really against it. This leads them to say some very unpleasant and dangerous things. It is in these practical and logical consequences of their thinking that the true nature of their campaign — which some of its partisans perhaps conceal from themselves or simply do not know — becomes clear.

I hope and pray that they (especially my brother) will one day choose differently, and I would be pleased if the case I make here helps them to do so. But I think it important for my opponents in this debate to recognize that it is a choice. The great metaphor of the Light of the World, standing at the door and knocking for admission, remains as true as it always was. In Holman Hunt's painting, there is no handle on Christ's side of the door. There never has been. There never will be.

But the new brand of militant atheism seems anxious to insist that there is no such choice. It adopts a mocking and high-handed tone of certainty, sneers at its Christian opponents, and states, or implies, that they must be stupid. This style of attack conforms to the irreverent spirit of the age and so is not very carefully examined. It is not widely recognized that secularism is a fundamentally political movement, which seeks to remove the remaining Christian restraints on power and the remaining traces of Christian moral law in the civil and criminal codes of the Western nations. It campaigns with increasing energy against the existence of specifically Christian state schools, not least because such schools are usually superior to their secular equivalents. It employs the cause of "equality" among sexual orientations to accomplish this, allocating the privileges of heterosexual marriage to homosexual civil partnership (and by implication, unmarried heterosexual couples) and so making them cease to be privileges. It makes it impossible for Christian churches to operate adoption societies, despite their effectiveness in this task, because it is no longer lawful for them to "discriminate" against homosexual couples who wish to adopt. It harasses and persecutes government employees who do not wish, on religious grounds, to solemnize homosexual unions. It compels the keepers of guest houses to welcome homosexual couples beneath their roofs, regardless of any moral objections they may have. It even punishes hospital nurses for offering to pray for their patients. All these things have taken place in Great Britain in recent years.

Secularism disingenuously disguises this restless reformism as a desire to be "left alone" by the religious. The religious would in fact happily leave atheists alone if not constantly under pressure to adapt their actions to atheist norms.

What is the real significance of this new and energetic movement? Is this something entirely new? Or is it something quite old, advancing under a new banner? Let us look further at the revealing fact of its reluctance to recognize the atheist elements of Communism.

PART 3

THE LEAGUE
OF THE
MILITANT GODLESS

Introduction

I promised earlier in the book that I would explain in more detail why I think it is absurd for my anti-theist brother to insist that the cruelty of Communist anti-theist regimes does not reflect badly on his case. After all, Soviet Communism used the same language, treasured the same hopes, and appealed to the same constituency as Western atheism does today.

Soviet power was, as it was intended to be, the opposite of faith in God. It was faith in the greatness of humanity and in the perfectibility of human society. The atheists cannot honestly disown it.

My brother Christopher suggests that Joseph Stalin's Soviet Union was in fact a religious state. The specifically anti-religious character of the Soviet system under Stalin makes such a claim nonsensical.

The chapters that follow provide a detailed response to this argument. They constitute the foundation of the answer to my brother's position. They are based on the most important direct experience of my life. When you have finished reading these chapters, I hope you will understand and share the urgency I feel about this matter.

CHAPTER 12

Fake Miracles
and Grotesque Relics

*"Set thou an ungodly man
to be ruler over him."*

(THE 109TH PSALM)

How the materialists like to jeer at the naïve faith of the peasant, fooled by relics, faith healers, and the general hocus-pocus of some branches of Christianity. As I am unmoved by alleged pieces of the True Cross or snippets of St. Bridget's fingernail, vials of liquefying blood, or mysterious cures at holy wells, this does not strike at the heart of my faith, though I do know people who take such things perfectly seriously, and I suspect — in spite of my robust English Protestantism — that miraculous healing does sometimes take place even in this skeptical age.

But the peasant's willingness to believe in such fancies is as nothing to the materialist intellectual's gullible open-mouthed willingness to believe anything. The biggest fake miracle staged in human history is the claim that Soviet Russia was a new civilization of equality, peace, love, truth, science, and progress.

Everyone now knows that it was a prison, a slum, a return to primitive barbarism, a kingdom of lies where scientists and doctors feared offending the secret police, and that its elite were corrupt and lived in secret luxury. I saw this myself firsthand when I lived there.

Yet it was the clever people, those who prided themselves on being unencumbered with superstition, those who viewed religion as a feature of the childhood of humanity, who fell for this swindle in the tens of thousands. The more educated and enlightened they were (by their own judgment, anyway), the more likely they were to be fooled. Some were deceived at a distance. Some were deceived after going there and somehow failing to notice what was going on. One correspondent of the *New York Times*, Walter Duranty, denied the existence of the great Ukrainian famine of 1932 – 33 even though he knew, directly and personally, that it was taking place. Others, who must have had their suspicions, willingly believed those denials and haughtily disbelieved truthful accounts of the misery that were published elsewhere by honest men and doubters of the Soviet miracle.

Denial of the existence of actual starvation, murder, persecution, and injustice seems to me to be much more distressing than believing that a wooden image of the Virgin Mary moved, when it did not, or seeing the face of Christ in a tree-stump, where it is not. Faith in the myth of progress can be just as strong as faith in God, though not necessarily so kind in its effects. At least the belief in miracles sometimes produces genuine cures. Lying about Leninism only abets murder and oppression.

A Mass of Self-Deceiving Lies

Any student of gullibility among the intelligent and worldly should study first of all the work of Sidney and Beatrice Webb on the Soviet Union. Their perfectly enormous book *Soviet Communism: A New Civilisation?* purports to be a respectable and carefully researched account of the USSR under Stalin. Its picture of a rational paradise of human progress is so wholly and completely false and can now be shown to be so at every turn by libraries full of records and by mountains of human skulls. Yet, on publication in the late 1930s it was generally greeted as a respectable work of scholarship and research. It is a sore shame that its authors did not live to see their work thoroughly shown up for what it was, a mass of self-deceiving lies. These lies served a filthy despotism, but perhaps more importantly encouraged the rational, materialist intellectuals of free nations in dangerous delusions, which still trouble us.

In realizing this, we need to remember that the Webbs were not themselves revolutionary Marxists or even former Trotskyists, but gentle Fabian social democrats, believers in lawful, democratic process, in the inevitability of gradualism, honorable in their personal dealings, honest according to their own lights. They were kind to their domestic servants, modest in their lives, studious, responsible, and serious, by no means stupid or ill-educated or personally callous. Nevertheless, thanks to their utopian opinions, they persuaded themselves (for instance) that the 1937 Moscow show trials were genuine criminal prosecutions. How could they have done that? These were state-sponsored stage-plays, transparently fictional. During these exhibitions, intelligent, educated men, formerly loyal servants of the Soviet regime, made unhinged confessions—after months of torture—to incredible catalogues of sabotage and conspiracy. Much of this was easily proved false at the time. All of it is now known to be untrue. The Webbs also once pronounced that the Central Executive Committee of the Soviet Communist Party, an assembly of lawless toadies and gangsters shivering in fear of the despot Stalin, "may not unfairly be regarded as corresponding to the [British] House of Commons." The House of Commons has suffered a severe loss of reputation in the years since this was written, but even so, this is a horrible slander on it.

The Webbs' successors live on today and share many of their attitudes, though they lack a proper fatherland to admire, to tell lies for, or to make fools of themselves over. Cuba, it is true, still just serves for some of them, and the strange continuing cult of Fidel Castro, in defiance of all facts, gives us a faint hint of what the Soviet delusion must have been like when it ruled the minds of so many. The reverence for the tyrant (invariably referred to as "Fidel," as if a personal friend) and the misrepresentation of his impoverished prison island as a paragon of medical and social achievement are examples of the power of self-deception interesting to any psychologist. But the wretched truth is too widely known, and Cuba is plainly sinking into the past, not striding into the future. China, ludicrously praised by gullible Westerners under the worst years of Mao Zedong, is now plainly a despotism and a police state. But because it is not a utopian despotism, foreign radicals are no longer willing to defend it. Regrettably, they see no need to apologize for their past praise, hoping that it will be forgotten.

Most of the people who would have apologized for Stalin in his day have now found other causes — the cultural and sexual revolution, campaigns to tax the Western poor to provide money for Africa's rich, and above all, the intolerant and puritan secular fundamentalism that gathers around the belief in manmade global warming. Others are devotees of the idea that the introduction of Western democracy into the Muslim world is possible. These beliefs allow their supporters to feel superior to others and to pursue a heaven on earth whose righteousness reflects on them. It is quite dangerous to challenge them, even though it is not dangerous at all to challenge Christianity or faith as a whole. The danger is not usually melodramatic or fatal, though it sometimes is. The climate change zealots (for example) issue no Fatwas, order no assassinations, and do not drag filmmakers from their bicycles and stab and behead them. They simply seek to drive their opponents from public debate by scorn, misrepresentation, and smears.

One of the fiercest orthodoxies of modern times was for a short while the state-sponsored cult of regime change that led to the Iraq invasion. The British weapons scientist David Kelly dared to cast doubt on the official justification for war in a confidential meeting with a journalist. Having been detected, he was exposed to interrogation and humiliation in public and soon afterward killed himself, presumably after intolerable pressure of some kind was put on him. This is perhaps the most frightening example of modern secular intolerance. But the facts later refuted that cult so utterly that — too late, alas, for Dr. Kelly and thousands of victims of the war — it lost its state-derived power to punish and marginalize.

The Homeless Utopians

The twenty-first-century successors of the Webbs can best be described as Homeless Utopians. They are sure there is no heaven, and they are coming to fear that there may be no earthly paradise either. But they continue, despite all previous failures, to hope for one. It may not offer them any great delights, but their faith enables them to feel superior to their neighbors. Holding tightly to the idea that what science cannot explain does not need explaining, they are still as ready as their fellow-traveling forebears were to slander the kingdom of heaven while mistakenly praising the fanciful utopias of man. They also like to believe that reason is all on their side.

The Webbs do us the great favor of explaining why people of this kind have always — at least in the years since the French Revolution — been so attracted to utopian states and to utopian movements and leaders. They declare that "it is exactly the explicit denial of the intervention of any God, *or indeed of any will other than human will* [my italics] in the universe, that has attracted to Soviet Communism, the sympathies of many intellectuals, and especially of scientists in civilised countries."

The Cult of "Science" in the USSR

The Webbs did express some very mild doubts about the Soviet system, but it is clear from their tone that they were exhilarated and inspired by explicit denial of God. It swept away one of the great obstacles they themselves faced in their own country. They plainly envied the Bolsheviks the freedom this gave them.

Consider this approving reference to the thoughts of Lenin — the absolute atheist, lover of violence, and begetter of the 1917 putsch — that brought the Russian Bolsheviks to power:

> Lenin insisted, as the basis of all his teaching, on a resolute denial of there being any known manifestation of the supernatural. He steadfastly insisted that the universe known to mankind (including mind equally with matter) was the sphere of science; and that this steadily advancing knowledge, the result of human experience of the universe, was the only useful instrument and the only valid guide of human action.... When the Bolsheviks came into power in 1917, they made this defiant and dogmatic atheism the basis of their action.[1]

Note the approval implied in the words "resolute," "steadfastly," and "defiant." The Webbs were impressed, even awed, by Lenin's renunciation of the spiritual.

Before discussing the suppression of religion, the Webbs explain, "So far we have described the positive and creative aspects of the cult of science in the USSR." (These include laudatory sections on such subjects as "The Leningrad Institute of the Brain" and "The Campaign against Rheumatism," which I commend to those with a strong sense of the ridiculous.)

---

1. This passage, and much of what follows, can be found in the second volume of the 1940 edition of their crowning work (published by Longmans, Green), as part of Chapter XI, entitled "Science the Salvation of Mankind." This is preceded by Chapter X, significantly called "The Remaking of Man." Presumably, they were correcting the final proofs as the Molotov-Ribbentrop Pact joined the USSR and the Third Reich in the most cynical military alliance in human history.

The Suppression of Religion

The Webbs creditably admit that "there is also a negative and destructive side: the violent denunciation and energetic uprooting, from one end of the Soviet Union to the other, of religion, and especially of the Christian religion." But there follow various denunciations of the evils of the Orthodox Church, tending to suggest that at least some of the attack on it was justified.

The Webbs go on to remark: "Whatever may have been the shortcomings and defects of the Greek Orthodox Church, it must be recognised that the attitude taken up by the Communist Party has excited a pained surprise and intense disapproval among earnest Christians in Western Europe and the United States, which has militated against any friendship with the USSR."

Note that they merely describe this surprise and disapproval among others (patronized as "earnest") rather than expressing it themselves. Surprise is "pained" and disapproval "intense." These are very different words from "resolute" and "steadfast." It appears that they regret the action (if they regret it at all) because it has damaged the image of a government they admire. They are not against it because it is bad in itself.

The Webbs' account of the Bolshevik state's persecution of religion, beginning on page 1007, is relentlessly complacent, self-deceiving, and defensive. They suggest without any good evidence that, following Lenin's *coup d'etat* of November 1917, there were "spontaneous mass conversions to atheism." They seek with painful diligence to avoid blaming the state for the killing of priests and the destruction of churches in the post-revolutionary period, attributing these events to "popular excesses," saying, "The Soviet government failed, for some years, to get control of the popular feeling" — although they also admit that this government "doubtless sympathised with it in all but its worst excesses." All but the worst? We shall see.

Teaching Religion to Children Banned

The Webbs' summary of the revolutionary campaign against the church is a useful starting point for examining this endless and ingenious fury, even so. This was not mere mindless smashing, intimidation, murder, and abuse, though there were plenty of these things. The Webbs correctly — and highly significantly — record that the schools were immediately secularized, religious teaching having been forbidden by Anatoly Lunacharsky's education decree on October 26, 1917, one of the very first broadly political acts of the Lenin putsch. There was then a second, still more devastating decree (on January 3, 1922), which utterly banned the teaching of religion to children, even singly, in churches, church buildings, or private homes.

Those who nowadays characterize the teaching of religion to children as a form of abuse — and I will come to that shortly — might be surprised to find their views so closely prefigured in this proclamation, which conceded that:

> Theological instruction for individuals over eighteen years of age who are able to discuss religious questions intelligibly can be authorised in special establishments opened by permission of the Soviet authorities.... Collective teaching

and isolated relations with young people under the age of eighteen, no matter where carried on, will be prosecuted with all the rigour of revolutionary law.

Such "rigour" could include the death penalty.

Rampant Anti-Christian Fervor

While Christian education was suppressed, official anti-Christian fervor was rampant. Hundreds of "Anti-God museums" appeared, mocking especially the Orthodox cult of relics, based on the belief that the corpses of saints did not decompose. Perhaps this is why, soon after, so much money and effort was used to try to prevent the corpse of Lenin from rotting, as if "science" could do what God could not. The Webbs once more assert, with their touching inability to understand the workings of Soviet despotism, that atheist propaganda was originally undertaken by individuals, only later supported by the weekly magazine *Bezbozhnik* ("The Godless"). Judging by the Webbs' account, this journal somehow seems to have just happened to be published — in a state where the Communist Party controlled every drop of ink, every ream of paper, every printing press, every train, every delivery van, and every newsstand.

Likewise, a conference, which just happened to be held in 1925 in a country where conferences were rather closely supervised by the secret police, just happened to adopt theses laying down the lines on which religion "should be combated." Coincidence is plainly hard at work in these matters, at least as far as the Webbs are concerned.

The mysterious passive voice is again in evidence as the Webbs record that a "Union of the Godless" was "established." At an "All-Union conference of Anti-religious Societies," which was somehow held in a country where every meeting hall was controlled by the state and a passport was necessary even for internal travel, this body changed its name to "The League of the Militant Godless."

The Webbs describe how very energetic campaigns for anti-religious propaganda were launched. (The passive voice appears yet again, as they strive to avoid the blazingly obvious truth that the state was engineering all these things.) And this movement somehow grew so that "From 9,000 cells and branches, it sprang year by year to 30,000, 50,000 and 70,000, with an aggregate membership, paying tiny fees, counted by millions."

Despite recording the mysterious flourishing of this body (coinciding as it did with confiscation of church property and execution, imprisonment, exile, and harassment of priests and believers), the Webbs go on, with the amazing self-delusion of the fellow traveler — to equate the position of Christians in the USSR with that of atheists in 1930s Britain:

> The social atmosphere in the USSR is unfriendly to any form of supernaturalism; just as the social atmosphere of the United States or Great Britain is unfriendly to any dogmatic atheism. But so far as the present writers could ascertain in 1932 and 1934, there is, in the USSR today, *nothing that can properly be called persecution* [my italics] of those who are Christians, any more than there is of Jews, Moslems or Buddhists. There is no law against the avowal of

belief in any religious creed, or the private practice of its rites. There is no exclusion from office of men or women who are believers.

The last claim was a gross untruth, while being narrowly and technically correct. The law did not bar believers from office as such. But open piety meant automatic expulsion from the Communist Party, which in turn meant exclusion from office. The Webbs — who may genuinely not have grasped this — add, equally reassuringly, "The Soviet government has more than once intervened to moderate the provocative activity of the Union of the Godless." Perhaps so. If its aim was to undermine Christian piety, its aggressive crudity was likely to have been counter-productive from time to time. The people were dis-tressed when jeering Bolsheviks lampooned the great festivals of Christmas and Easter in the city streets. The Socialist G. P. Fedotov recalled meeting one such procession:

> The population, and not only the faithful, looked upon this hideous carnival with dumb horror. There were no protests from the silent streets — the years of terror had done their work — but nearly everyone tried to turn off the road when they met this shocking procession.... The parade moved along empty streets and its attempts at creating laughter or provocation were met with dull silence on the part of the occasional witnesses.

Despite an attempt in 1923 by more intelligent Bolsheviks to restrain this kind of persecution by mockery, it returned later with renewed force under the direction of the regime's chief

God-baiter, Emelian Yaroslavski. A state that controls the waking lives of the rising generations can in fact erase faith by the use of relentless strength and consistency. And that is what happened.

The Bolshevik leadership genuinely hated and despised the thing they sought to destroy. A fair example of the league's later propaganda is a 1929 issue of *Bezbozhnik* showing two smirking workers dumping Jesus Christ, open-mouthed and goggling, from a red wheelbarrow on to a garbage heap, along with some empty wine bottles. Behind them, a third proletarian is energetically smashing a church bell with a hammer. In the background, vast factory chimneys — the spires of Communism — pour soot into a vacant socialist heaven. The caption urges workers to abandon the old, allegedly drunken religious holiday of the Transfiguration and instead celebrate "Industrialization Day." Much more offensive and sometimes obscene imagery was often used by this organization, whose pornographic and shocking parodies of religious ceremonies were an echo of the "Worship of Reason" in the French Revolution, when prostitutes dressed as Reason were paraded in churches.

Priests almost invariably appear in *Bezbozhnik*'s cartoons and posters as sinister drunks. (One interestingly appears in the same form in the work of the modern anti-Christian British children's writer Philip Pullman.) Religious grandmothers, an enemy who could not easily be stifled even in a totalitarian state, are portrayed as crow-like witches trying to entice children into dark ecclesiastical portals; scavenger birds sit on the roofs of decrepit churches, while nearby the new enlightened state school shines with the virtue of science. The Almighty himself is portrayed as a red-nosed old booby in thick spectacles, wearing a White Guard cap and smoking a cigar. A particularly brutal cartoon depicts the Last Supper as a boozy debauch. Two of the apostles are under the table; bottles roll on the floor of the Upper Room; disciples reel, leer, or brawl with each other, haloes akimbo. Jesus — bottle in one hand, glass in the other — is depicted as saying (I translate fairly freely): "Drink ye all of this, for this is my own bathtub hooch, which is being drunk for you, for us and for many. Hurrah!" An explanatory text claims that the "so-called 'Last Supper'" clearly proves that religion establishes, proclaims, and morally excuses drunkenness. "To fight against religion is to fight against drunkenness."

The anti-drinking message is strong, as shown in that blasphemous lampoon of the Last Supper, and is an attempt to bracket the church with a tragedy that has always been the plague of the Russian poor. Yet, as I observed myself seventy years later, long after the war against Christianity had been effectively won, drunkenness was still a dreadful scourge across Russia, defying all attempts to suppress it. The main effect of a ban on alcohol sales, in 1990 Moscow, was a grave shortage of sugar, which had all been used to make moonshine vodka. Public and private drunkenness continued at appalling levels, as anyone could readily observe, wrecking family life and poisoning a society already in great pain. Far from providing a new materialist type of man with liberation from drink and ignorance, the "new civilization" left him more enslaved to alcohol than before and deprived of hope in either this world or the next.

CHAPTER 13

Provoking a Bloody War with the Church

"Then let mine enemy persecute my soul, and take me:
yea, let him tread my life down upon the earth,
and lay mine honour in the dust."

(THE 7TH PSALM)

Vladimir Ilyich Lenin's secret Shuya Memorandum of March 22, 1922, launched the state-sponsored looting of Russia's churches in the hope of provoking the Orthodox hierarchy into resistance and so crushing them. "In order to get our hands on this fund of several hundred million gold rubles (and perhaps even several hundred billion), we must do whatever is necessary," commanded the Bolshevik leader, whose tone was as ever shockingly bloodthirsty and violent. "We must now give the most decisive and merciless battle to the Black Hundreds[1] clergy and subdue its resistance with such brutality that they will not forget it for decades to come." But the Bolshevik

---

1. The "Black Hundreds" were a semi-official militia that engaged in state-sponsored pogroms against Jews. Some clergymen supported this despicable organization, but many did not. Some leaders of the "Living Church," which for a while collaborated with the Bolsheviks, had been open supporters of it. The use of the phrase in the memorandum is in general a smear.

expectations of gold from this source were absurdly ambitious and probably a red herring from the start. The real motive was to goad Christians into defending themselves and then to smash them in pieces. In this it succeeded. That year, 2,691 priests, 1,962 monks, and 3,447 nuns were killed.[2]

No wonder William Henry Chamberlin, in his account of what he saw during twelve years as a correspondent in Moscow for the *Christian Science Monitor*, wrote: "There have been many instances in history when one religion cruelly persecuted all others; *but in Russia the world is witnessing the first effort to destroy completely any belief in supernatural interpretation of life* [my italics]."[3]

Chamberlin compares Communism with religion, describing it as "the faith without God." But he stresses the difference between the two: "What distinguishes Communism from the fanatical authoritarian religions with which it has so many points in common is of course its rigid, dogmatic and uncompromising exclusion of any element in life lying outside the confines of the present material world.... Truth and objectivity are of minor importance. The main purpose is to defame and denounce in every way."

Chamberlin notes that until 1929, Article 4 of the Soviet constitution guaranteed a "right to religious propaganda" as well as the right to anti-religious propaganda. After that date, the faithful were only allowed to "profess" their faith, not to propagandize for it. But the Godless kept their right to campaign.

Priests and their families were subject to severe persecution.

---

2. See Stéphane Courtois et al., *The Black Book of Communism: Crimes, Terror, Repression* (Cambridge, MA: Harvard University Press, 1999), 91.
3. *Russia's Iron Age* (Boston: Little, Brown, 1935), 311.

A priest's children were barred from middle or higher schools or from state employment unless they renounced and broke off all connections with their fathers. Priests were disenfranchised along with criminals and the insane. They were also denied ration cards, often necessary for survival in periods of shortage.

Chamberlin also details the Communist campaign against Christmas, a festival that — because it is so much loved by children — arouses the special hostility of utopian despots at all times and in all places. Pointing out that the sale of Christmas trees was then strictly forbidden in Moscow (except to foreigners in special hard-currency shops), Chamberlin quotes from a little pamphlet aimed at schoolchildren, "Against the Christmas Tree." This publication was one in a series called "The Library of the Young Atheist," whose time has plainly almost come around again. It contains this severe warning:

> Millions of little children are brought up by very religious grandmothers. For such children the Christmas tree represents a very great danger.... Not one Young Pioneer detachment, not one school and not one group of Young Atheists should leave children of pre-school age unattended during the Christmas holidays. The struggle against the Christmas Tree is the struggle against religion and against our class enemies.

By the time I lived in Moscow at the very end of the Communist era, sixty years later, few had any knowledge or memory of Christmas as it had once been celebrated. Trees were sold in street markets, but they were not Christmas trees; they were for the wholly secular New Year festival, which was by then the principal winter holiday. Christmas was more or less dead. Middle-aged, middle-class Russians generally viewed religion with a sour contempt taught to them repeatedly since their earliest childhood.

Children, rather nauseatingly described as "our only privileged class," were encouraged to place more trust in the state than in their families, not least by the odious cult of Pavlik Morozov, a peasant child said to have been killed by his grandfather after he denounced his own parents to the NKVD (secret police) for hoarding grain. Morozov may well not have existed, but the mythology surrounding him was extensive, including visits by school children to statues of him. One such statue was still to be seen in a small park in the Krasnaya Presnya district of Moscow as late as 1991. It vanished soon after the final collapse of Communism in that year, but several adult Russians known to me recalled being taught to revere him, and one visibly shuddered at the memory, though she was in all other ways a devoted and loyal Communist.

The Destruction of Beauty and Custom

Perhaps the greatest damage done to religion by systematic state persecution was to break the continuity of tradition and prayer. A famous story was told in 1990s Moscow of a group of children of elite Russians, members of the privileged Nomenklatura, who, realizing in their early twenties that they were Jews, decided to celebrate Yom Kippur — a solemn holy day set aside for atonement and repentance — with a large and joyous party. This utter ignorance of any religious lore and traditions was common.

Although plenty of Russians, including leading Communists, had been secretly baptized by devout grandmothers, few had any knowledge of the church seasons, rituals, or scriptures. There were some isolated believers, but they were not in any way typical. The link between the people and their Christian inheritance — in custom, seasons, traditions, music, and belief — had been effectively broken, and Christianity had been reduced to a private matter, much as it is in Muslim nations. Moscow, despite growing enormously in the seventy-five years since the Bolshevik putsch, had lost 500 of its 600 churches, many of them spitefully desecrated, some blown up, some relegated to serve as store-rooms or used as reformatories for feral delinquent youths who were encouraged to befoul and desecrate them. Any serious career was closed to an observant believer, since (as mentioned above) church membership was explicitly incompatible with Communist Party membership. For decades, spies were assumed to be present in all congregations. It was hard to see how Holy Russia could ever recover.

Since then, there has been much rebuilding, re-gilding of old domes, and ostentatious religious observance by the powerful and the rich. The Kremlin cathedrals and St. Basil's in Red Square (where I attended an almost ecstatic celebration of Easter in 1992, the first in that building for many decades) have been brought back into use. But I do not think that what was lost has been recovered, and I suspect it never will be.

The persistence of some Communist symbolism in the state — the huge crystal red stars on the Kremlin towers, the unburied corpse of Lenin in Red Square — have little if anything to do with socialism. But they show that in a de-Christianized society, the state still has to rely on the childhood indoctrination of millions of citizens for a large part of its authority. If the church and tradition had not been so completely erased, these things would not be needed. Perhaps, two generations from now, Lenin will finally receive decent burial and the red stars will at last be taken down. But the church is unlikely to fill the space from which it was so violently expelled in the Communist period.

Systematic Malice

The Bolsheviks, who erased most of their original opponents with appalling violence, were from the start more subtle about religion, an enemy they knew was stronger than it looked. In his passionate yet restrained book *The Russian Crucifixion,* published in 1930, F. A. Mackenzie lists the provisions of the People's Commissariat decree on religious associations issued on April 8, 1929. This was an extension of Lunacharsky's original anti-religious decree set out on January 23, 1918, which had ended the teaching of religion in schools, had disestablished the church, and had begun the official state campaign against God. Much thought had gone into this web of regulations. Its systematic, cunning malice is as frightening as naked violence.

Its authors knew exactly where and how to strike, how to bind, and what limits would be most effective in achieving what they wished to bring about. Each religious society had to be registered; a person might only belong to one such organization (so a church member could not also belong to the YMCA or a Student Christian group). Religious societies might only use one building for worship. Outside preachers were banned. Churches could not use their property for any purposes but religious ones. They could not give charity to outsiders or their own members.

The state must have a monopoly of welfare. Special meetings for women, children, or adolescents were banned; likewise, Bible study groups, book groups, sewing groups, organized excursions, children's playgrounds, libraries or reading rooms, or any kind of medical assistance. Religious symbols were banned from public buildings. Processions and open-air services were banned.

Secular Intolerance

There were no private schools under the Communist regime. All education was under the control of the Communist state. Mackenzie quotes the generally gullible newspaper, the *Manchester Guardian* (now the *Guardian*), as having maintained that "anti-religious education consists in simple teaching in the natural sciences." He then quotes, in devastating rebuttal, Susan Lawrence, a British Labour politician, who might have been expected to be sympathetic to the Communists. She reported from Moscow in 1923:

> The schools are as I have said propaganda schools, framed to inculcate a definite ideal both in politics and religion. Communism is to be taught and religion is to be exterminated, and the whole programme of the schools is to be directed towards these ends. Exactly as the lessons in revolutionary history, and elementary economics, have as their object establishing firmly the outlook on the world of say [Thomas] Huxley or Mr [Charles] Bradlaugh [two prominent British atheists].
>
> It follows, as is always the case with dogmatic education,

that there can be no free play of thought, and in particular there is no room in the system for any teacher who does not think as the State does. A teacher who was not a Communist or who was a professing Christian I am pretty sure would have to hide his opinion or lose his job as certainly as would be the case with a convinced atheist in a Catholic school in England.

Lawrence does not make the important point that in Britain's more pluralist society such a dissenter would have a chance of working elsewhere, whereas in Soviet Russia he would probably starve, if he remained at liberty and alive at all.

Mackenzie then describes the discussions in professional magazines for Soviet teachers of how best to destroy the religious instinct among children. God and Christ must be treated as equivalent to fairytale figures, ghosts, and goblins. The church's wealth is then to be discussed, and the point made that it would be better spent on repairing roads or buying shoes for children. Saintliness is to be debunked and associated with fraud and fakery. It is alleged that diphtheria can be spread by eating the Host at Communion and even that the Easter Kiss may spread syphilis.

All this time the young are under great pressure to join mixed-sex Communist youth leagues — which are of course most active on Sundays when church services are being held. Mackenzie states, "They are soaked in Marxism; they are taught Communist songs and sing them as they march along, they are taught to hate priests; in country towns when they see one they hoot at him."

Mackenzie then notes:

The summer and autumn of 1929 witnessed a steady growth of Communist aggression.... everything short of the actual closing of the churches seemed now to have been done, but here the ingenuity of the Party in power proved not yet to be exhausted. The government decreed a five-day week in the place of the seven-day week, in order to break completely the observance of Sunday. Each person is now to have one day off in five, but since the day varies according to each person's work, different members of a family often have their periodical rest on different days.

The Bolsheviks had clearly learned from the failure of the ten-day week that formed part of the French Revolutionary calendar. This collapsed largely because the Sabbath of Reason came around much less often than the Sabbath of Christianity. But even the Bolsheviks' five- (and later six-) day week experiment eventually proved too unpopular to sustain, because it made life too miserable.

Mackenzie records:

There came a campaign of the confiscation of church bells, nominally in order that their metal might be used for industrial purposes, but really to stop the call of religion. The workers were given the power to initiate proceedings to close churches, and in large sections of the country they launched campaigns to stop by force every place of worship there.... the economic regulations were specially used to penalise the priests. From all over the country accounts began to arrive of the arrests of priests, because they had not produced the quantity of grain required, or had not been able to meet high taxes.

Persecution of Christianity
Was Not Hidden

Mackenzie — who lived in Communist Russia for three years from 1921 to 1924 and plainly had extensive personal contact with many religious Russians — also gives detailed accounts of cruel and unjust imprisonment and executions, a detailed exposition of conditions at the Solovyetsky concentration camp and of several other prisons, convincing accounts of miserable exiles and other cruel punishments.

It is important to note here that these harrowing descriptions — which probably err on the side of mildness — came long before anyone had heard of Alexander Solzhenitsyn or the Gulag Archipelago. Yet information about the expanding network of cruel and miserable prison camps was surprisingly freely available, especially concerning the island prison at Solovyetsky. The Soviet state had already quite obviously laid the foundations of the repressive apparatus that Stalin would perfect. Details of these facts were published and available throughout the long years when the Webbs and many others in the democratic and legal Western Left were prepared to defend the Soviet Union as a worthy social experiment and perhaps more. The Webbs cite Mackenzie in their bibliography, but they plainly regard him as an exaggerator. Time (whose daughter is Truth) is on his side.

For those who wished to know, there was extensive evidence of the terrorist savagery of the Soviet state from very early on. The main barrier to such knowledge lay in the minds of those who idealized the Soviet state and did not wish to hear or believe it. It is also important to say that major figures in the religious resistance to the Bolsheviks, such as the judicially murdered Metropolitan Benjamin and Patriarch Tikhon, who was terrorized into self-abasement, were by no means mere reactionary tools of the old regime's indefensible Holy Synod. Benjamin was explicitly in favor of separation of church and state. Tikhon came to prominence only after the collapse of the old regime and pointedly did not ally himself with the counter-revolutionary movement known as the Whites. But both were undoubtedly opposed to the extraordinarily violent version of socialism that burst unexpectedly onto the country after Lenin stepped from his train in Petrograd. Some of the leading figures in the pro-Bolshevik "Living Church," by contrast, had been keen Monarchists and supporters of the "Black Hundreds," state sponsored anti-Jewish organizations that often launched pogroms. One had spread the Blood Libel (that Jews used Christian blood in Passover bread) as recently as 1913.

Even more vital is this point: The course of the Bolshevik government is a very varied one. It was merciless to its early political enemies, whether they were Czarist-era reformers, supporters of Alexander Kerensky, or fellow revolutionaries and socialists who rejected the Vanguard Party. But this was a brief frenzy, and they were all very soon either dead or imprisoned or fled abroad. The Bolsheviks killed their own most loyal supporters at Kronstadt in 1921, because they failed to understand that the revolution no longer required revolutionaries, but obedient servants. It resorted to the New Economic Policy when it was necessary for survival and abandoned it equally swiftly when it was no longer needed. It accepted foreign famine aid at one point and left millions to starve a few years later, when it wished to exterminate a whole social class.

The government veered between ultra-radical social policies

on such matters as abortion and homosexuality, adopted in the 1920s, and highly conservative attitudes on the same issues, adopted in 1934 (to the confusion of the revolution's Western "progressive" supporters). It would then once again reverse its position on abortion, which by the 1990s was the main form of contraception in the USSR. It sought expansion by foreign wars, then preached socialism in one country, then began a new wave of socialist imperialism that would take it to Berlin, Prague, and Vienna at its highest point. It turned, cannibal-like, upon its own ranks and upon the entire Russian people in terrible purges whose extent will never be fully known and whose secret victims were still being discovered in shallow, unmarked graves in city center parks and gardens during my years in Moscow. Then it abandoned this and denounced those responsible. The government despised Hitler, then courted him, then despised him again. But during all this period, it consistently and without let-up sought to wipe out the teaching of faith and of the worship of God among children.

Anatoly Lunacharksy was the first to begin persecution, subtle but deadly, in his education decree. In my days as a Trotskyist, he was regarded as an enlightened, almost gentle intellectual figure, the kind of revolutionary who remained respectable because he had later been denounced by Stalin. We used to sell his book, *Revolutionary Silhouettes*, on our bookstalls. The persecution was vigorously supported by both Leon Trotsky and Vladimir Lenin, both of whom (for all their other differences) were enthusiastic anti-theists and neither of whom can be accused of seeking to set up Communism as a religion (though Trotsky, realizing the power of religion, did seek to appropriate the rites of passage formerly celebrated by the church).

When Stalin wiped Lunacharksy from Soviet history in his great purge, he did not do so because the former Education Commissar had been hostile to the church. When Stalin revived patriotism and slightly relaxed the persecution of the adult church (though not the much more important efforts to destroy its roots among the young) during the 1941 – 45 war against Germany, he did not do so because he had all along been secretly longing to do so. Rather, he did this because both forces might serve his desperate ends. Stalin's successor, Nikita Sergeyevich Khrushchev — likewise a man who was cruel when it was practical, and enlightened when that was practical, in accordance with revolutionary ethics — was to launch a particularly merciless assault on the church in the years after the war.

The regime's institutional loathing for the teaching of religion, and its desire to eradicate it, survived every doctrinal detour and swerve. And the eradication campaign — unlike so many of its other campaigns — was a success, perhaps because it required only destruction. Soviet power only failed when it tried to build or create. The very limited religious revival of Christianity in the new Russia is one of buildings, ritual, and status. God is largely absent from the hearts of the people, who know little of him and were not introduced to him at the age when (as the commissars knew and the new anti-theists know) we learn to love ideas as well as people. If we do not learn faith then, it is unlikely we shall ever learn it. If we do learn it then, we are unlikely ever to shake it off, though we are afraid to do so. So it is important that what we learn should be good. So what is good? Was the anti-theist teaching of the Soviet schools good? Did they produce a good society? Was Homo Sovieticus, the new human ideal of Communism, a triumph? Nobody who ever visited that country with open eyes could think so.

It is conceivable that Russia's future generations may rediscover what their great-grandparents knew. It is certain that those born and raised in the Soviet period are with very few exceptions closed to the ideas of God and conscience as understood by faithful Christians blessed with a religious upbringing in a Christian culture. This may be especially the case with those in authority who now ostentatiously adopt religious postures because they realize that their country's reserves of moral authority are quite spent. But the Godless emptiness helps to explain why post-Communist Russia has struggled so hard to cope with unaccustomed liberty and has gone so rapidly from being a thought-police state to being a gangster state, with an interlude of chaos in between.

CHAPTER 14

The Great Debate

"Behold, they speak with their mouth,
and swords are in their lips."

(THE 59TH PSALM)

Let us now dispose of the claim made by my brother Christopher, which I tried to challenge during our debate in Grand Rapids, Michigan, on April 3, 2008, that "Communist absolutists did not so much negate religion, in societies that they well understood were saturated with religion, as seek to replace it."[1]

First, an interesting reflection on the title of his book in the USA, where "God" was rendered as "god" on the cover and title page — different from the British edition. In Decree Number 176 of the Revolutionary Government, issued in 1917, a number of spelling reforms were introduced by law, including the abolition of several letters in the Cyrillic alphabet. The decree also stated that the word *god* should henceforth be used without a capital "G."

The coincidence in instinct, taste, and thought between my

---

1. *God Is Not Great* (New York: Twelve, 2007), 246.

brother and the Bolsheviks and their sympathizers is striking and undeniable. I wish he would talk about it more. As an ex-Trotskyist myself, I have watched and listened in frustration as others, who do not know how and what revolutionaries think, fail to press the key questions. Christopher remains equivocal about Leon Trotsky. He recently nominated this blood-encrusted putschist conspirator and apostle of revolutionary terror as his subject for an edition of the BBC's radio series "Great Lives," in which the guest argues for the greatness of a chosen individual. During a recent TV encounter with Robert Service, Trotsky's biographer,[2] Christopher interestingly praised Trotsky for his "moral courage." It is doubtful (see p. 158) if Trotsky could himself have accepted this compliment. In both these broadcasts, the issue of whether Trotsky's unvaryingly repressive instincts and actions cancel out his skills as polemicist and journalist — and ought to deny him greatness — was not fully resolved.

Christopher has also said, "One of Lenin's great achievements, in my opinion, is to create a secular Russia."[3] Alas, the interviewer does not seem to have inquired what Lenin's other "great achievements" were, or if he did, the answers have not been recorded. Nor was there any discussion about the methods Lenin used to achieve this end. Lenin certainly did create a secular Russia, but how does this accord with my brother's claim that the Communists also sought to replace religion, not to negate it?

Many Russians of my acquaintance would not use the words

---

2. Uncommon Knowledge, "National Review Online" (August 2009), http://tv.nationalreview.com/uncommonknowledge. See Service, *Trotsky: A Biography* (Cambridge, MA: Harvard University Press/Belknap Press, 2009).
3. In a PBS interview for the "Heaven on Earth" series, 2005.

"great" or "achievement" to describe any of this bloodthirsty, duplicitous, and spiteful tyrant's actions, unless treason in collusion with a foreign enemy, destruction, desecration, persecution, murder, and extreme pitilessness can be described as achievements, or the creation and consolidation of the world's most effective and ruthless repressive apparatus can be presented as "great." But we cannot all be of one mind, and unless there is an absolute standard of good and evil, I suppose we have to suspend judgment on the broken eggs (and the broken lives) until we can be sure that there will be no omelet. And even then, we may be indulgent on the grounds that the omelet might have been a good one, if only it had not been for so many events beyond the cook's control.

Or so I have often heard it argued, in various Marxist-Leninist covens whose devotees have gone on to be model citizens in the Politically Correct state. I happen to think that there is an absolute standard of good and evil, so I would have to lament over the broken eggs even if there were an omelet instead of a bloody mess.

It would be crude and false to identify my brother as some kind of fellow traveler of the Bolshevik regime. He has more sense than to be such a thing. And that, emphatically, is not my charge. Yet, is there perhaps a vestigial sympathy with the great experiment and a far-from-vestigial loathing for those things it extirpated — monarchy, tradition, patriotism, and faith?

Sentimental for Socialism?

In the encounter with Robert Service mentioned above, my brother speaks of the (undoubted) wickedness of the White counter-revolutionary armies. He suggests that the 1905 Russian Revolution might have produced happier results had socialism triumphed then. But Russia in 1905 was one of the most rapidly growing industrial countries in human history, acquiring a middle class and seeking energetically to reform itself. It was precisely this development of a giant rival in the East that Imperial Germany — which instigated and financed Lenin's putsch — feared. If the 1914 war had never happened, Russia might have become happy, prosperous, and free, peacefully and without cataclysm. The Communists only came to power because of the demoralization of war and because they were hired by the Kaiser's General Staff to get Russia out of the war.

We have to wonder if some sentimental belief that socialism might have succeeded under other leadership still lingers in my brother's mind. Trotskyism is, at bottom, the self-delusion that it could all have turned out otherwise under a more intelligent, literate leader. There is no actual evidence for this at all — and plenty to the contrary. It is pure wish-fulfillment. I say this as a former Trotskyist, who managed to delude himself in this way for some years.[4] It is a mechanism for avoiding the unwanted truth that socialism failed not because it was badly led or unlucky, but because it was wrong. And it is a means for avoiding the further conclusion — even more frightening — that it failed because it sought to render unto Caesar the things that belong to God.

Does my brother yearn for an alternative history in which

---

4. A description of my departure from this view can be found in my 2009 book *The Broken Compass*.

socialism succeeded, "hoping it might be so" like the disillusioned Thomas Hardy in *The Oxen*, yearning for belief in the
old story that the animals kneel on Christmas Eve? In 1920,
when the nature of the Soviet regime was as yet not fully clear
and its supposed glories were not yet drowned in blood, many
prominent atheist intellectuals were impressed with the rationalism and science-worship of the new state.

Bertrand Russell wrote rather candidly in 1920 that he had
gone to Russia "believing himself to be a Communist" — but
after meeting Lenin and Trotsky he had the sense to say that
"contact with those who have no doubts has intensified a thou-
sandfold my own doubts, not only of communism, but of every
creed so firmly held that for its sake men are willing to inflict
widespread misery."[5]

But others, especially the English Fabians, were not so easily
put off and liked what they saw. Recall the way Beatrice and Sidney Webb so interestingly put it: "It is exactly the explicit denial
of the intervention of any God, or indeed of any will other than
human will in the universe, that has attracted to Soviet Communism, the sympathies of many intellectuals, and especially of
scientists in civilised countries."

Is it perhaps this ambiguity toward the great Bolshevik
experiment that makes my brother unwilling to look the anti-
theism of the Communists in the face and recognize it as his
kin? Is it perhaps this unwillingness that impels him to maintain that one of the most anti-theist states in history was in fact
itself a form of theism? Let us go further.

---

5. *The Nation* (July 31, 1920).

The Personality Cult of the Stalinists versus the Living Church

My brother argues that the personality cult of the Stalinists was itself a religion:

> The solemn elevation of infallible leaders who were a source of endless bounty and blessing; the permanent search for heretics and schismatics; the mummification of dead leaders as icons and relics; the lurid show trials that elicited incredible confessions by means of torture … none of this was very difficult to interpret in traditional terms.[6]

This is an elegant evasion of the point. Had their only concern been a need for a belief system that prostrated itself before them, the Bolsheviks did in fact have to handle the body known as the "Living Church" (see chap. 13). This group of collaborationists was composed of priests and bishops who were more than ready to place Orthodox Christianity at the disposal of the Council of People's Commissars. But after having served the Bolsheviks by splitting and weakening the Orthodox Church, the leaders of the Living Church were arrested (and presumably murdered in prison, since no more was heard of them) in the early 1930s. The same thing happened to their Jewish equivalents, the "Yevseksiy" (Jewish sections of the Communist Party). These were wound up in 1929, their functionaries purged in 1937. In this case it is recorded that their chairman, Semyon Dimanshtein, was shot in captivity.

The rulers of the cowed and submissive church during Sta-

---

6. *God Is Not Great* (New York: Twelve, 2007), 246.

lin's wartime relaxation (and afterward) were also placemen of the regime, penetrated by the secret police and pitifully willing to abase themselves in return for survival. But they were called on for help only when the state was in such peril from the armies of Hitler that it had to evacuate its capital to Kuibyshev (and the mummy of Lenin to Tyumen) in 1941. Visitors to Moscow can still see the monument marking the Germans' farthest advance into the city outskirts, a line of gigantic Dragons' Teeth in what is now the suburb of Khimki, shockingly close to Red Square. Stalin genuinely and rightly feared defeat and humiliating death. Without that terror, he would never have called on the church.

Many of the clergy and church members, having been the slaves of the Tsars, would no doubt have been ready to make terms with the new government if they had been given the chance to do so. I noted earlier that among the leaders of the Living Church were creatures of this sort. Their discreditable record during the old regime (which I for one make no attempt to deny) showed that they were corruptible. Such a concordat would have been considerably easier and quicker than the course the Bolsheviks did in fact adopt. But no such thing took place. Instead — under the Carthaginian peace of Brest-Litovsk, during civil war, during the unsuccessful invasion of Poland and the defeat that resulted, during the great famines, and even during their death-grapple with the Third Reich — the Communist authorities continued to try to stop the teaching of the Gospels to children, to mock and harry the celebration of Christmas, and to drive the very idea of God out of the national mind. They may, from time to time, have been happy for the people to revere the dead Lenin or the living Stalin, but it was not central to their propaganda. In my time in Moscow, when Marxism-Leninism had run down like an unwound clock and was barely function-ing, the mummy of Lenin was no more than a tourist curiosity. The local cinema bore poet-playwright Vladimir Mayakovsky's famous pseudo-religious slogan, "Lenin lived, Lenin lives, Lenin will live!" although I do not think anyone took the second two declarations literally or even metaphorically.

But never at any stage were the Communist authorities will-ing to allow children in their care to revere Christ born, Christ crucified, and Christ risen. And they never relented from their ultimate aim of installing a wholly materialist, scientist con-sciousness in the minds of the people under their rule.

Intelligent revolutionaries are always most interested in the young. They know that the ideas and characters of mature adults are generally fully formed and cannot easily be changed, though they can be expensively and painfully terrified, suborned, and cajoled into acting against those ideas. But they also know that, if they can control the schools and the youth movements, they can stamp out unwelcome beliefs in a generation or two.

Adolf Hitler at one stage told his opponents that they might rage at him if they wished but he did not care, because their children would, in a few years, be his and not theirs. "When an opponent declares, 'I will not come over to your side,' I say calmly, 'Your child belongs to us already.... What are you? You will pass on. Your descendants, however, now stand in the new camp. In a short time they will know nothing but this new com-munity.'"[7] Stalin and Mussolini similarly took a great deal of trouble over the young. There were things they did not want them to know or to hear.

---

7. From a speech on November 6, 1933.

Is Religion Child Abuse?

It is notable that my brother's work and that of Richard Dawkins[8] coincide closely on one striking point. My brother devotes a chapter to the question "Is religion child abuse?" Amid a multitude of fulminations about circumcision, masturbation, and frightening children with stories of hell, he lets slip what I suspect is his actual point: "If religious instruction were not allowed until the child had attained the age of reason, we would be living in a quite different world." This is perfectly true, as is his earlier statement that "the obsession with children, and with rigid control over their upbringing, has been part of every system of absolute authority." There is a revealing assumption buried in these statements and also in the opening part of the chapter, in which he says, "We can be sure that religion has always hoped to practise upon the unformed and undefended minds of the young, and has gone to great lengths to make sure of this privilege by making alliances with secular powers in the material world." Does he realize that he is here describing Soviet Communism?

There is something tellingly odd and incomplete about this statement. Religion is most generally introduced to children, not by the state but by their own parents, who love them and believe that faith will benefit them.[9] This most certainly happened before there were any schools even in advanced countries. In Britain, the churches created schools (where attendance was

---

8. *The God Delusion* (London: Bantam Press, 2006).
9. It is interesting that this was not the case in either Christopher's childhood or mine, in which religion was always associated with school and authority rather than with our home.

voluntary) before the state did, and the political battle between state and church over who should control these schools continues to this day. In the USA, the public schools were set up in many cases as a secular "American" counter to Roman Catholic parochial schools. The American home schooling movement exists mainly because parents, not churches, and certainly not the state, desire a religious upbringing for their young that the state is not willing to provide.

Therefore, in two of the freest countries of the world, the claim that the church has sought to keep the privilege of education by making alliances with the secular power is much less than the whole truth. In totalitarian states, by contrast, either the church has been forced into such arrangements through Concordats and suffered as a result, or it has been brusquely ordered from the schools and loaded with restrictions designed to undermine domestic religion and indeed attack the family itself.

In *The God Delusion*, Richard Dawkins still allows the deity his initial capital letter, but he too has a lengthy section on "Physical and Mental Abuse."[10] He recounts how "in the question time after a lecture in Dublin, I was asked what I thought about the widely publicized cases of sexual abuse by Catholic priests in Ireland. I replied that, horrible as sexual abuse no doubt was, the damage was arguably less than the long-term psychological damage inflicted by bringing the child up Catholic in the first place." Dawkins has repeated these sentiments on several other occasions. For instance, he declared on the "Sunday Edition," a British TV program, "What I really object to is — and I think it's actually abusive to children — is to take a tiny child and say 'You are a Christian child or you are a Muslim

10. Page 315.

child.' I think it is wicked if children are told 'You are a member of such and such a faith simply because your parents are.'"

The word *abuse* used here by both Richard Dawkins and my brother is far stronger than it first seems to be. In modern Britain and slightly less so in the USA, an accusation of "child abuse" is devastating to the accused. It is almost universally assumed to be true. Juries and the media are instantly prejudiced against the defendant before any evidence has been heard. To suggest that any person so charged may be innocent is to risk being accused of abuse oneself. It has been suggested to me by several correspondents that the charge has often been used by women in divorce cases in order to secure custody of the children, because it is so effective in achieving this, in that it instantly turns the balance against the accused man.

To use the expression "child abuse" in this context — of religious education by parents or teachers — is to equate such education with a universally hated crime. Such language prepares the way for intolerance and, quite possibly, legal restrictions on the ability of parents to pass on their faith to their children, just as they are increasingly restricted in disciplining them. If Professor Dawkins genuinely believes what he said to the Dublin audience, then he should logically believe that "bringing the child up Catholic" should be a criminal offense attracting a long term of imprisonment and public disgrace. If he does not mean this, what does he mean by the use of such wildly inflated language, and what is he trying to achieve by it?

And what is my brother doing, coincidentally asking "Is Religion Child Abuse?" in his competing anti-theist volume? Interestingly, he does not really answer his own inquiry. The chapter, promising a bold answer to a bold question, never delivers what it seems to offer. It drains away into some ramblings on the subject of evolution, circumcision, masturbation, and the actual sexual abuse of children by Roman Catholic priests. I will not be trapped into defending *them*; their actions were atrocious, particularly because of who and what they were, and the Roman Catholic Church has been feeble in dealing with them. But it can hardly be claimed that they were the only people ever to abuse children sexually or cover it up, or that they were in any way following the dictates of their church. In fact, most of this abuse involves homosexual assaults on pubescent boys, of the kind (not remotely connected with religion) that occurred at my private school. This fact is neglected at least partly because it is no longer respectable to disapprove of homosexuality as such, and many homosexual liberationists campaign for ever-lower ages of consent — which would bring such offenses perilously close to being legal, especially given the feebleness with which the current age of consent is policed. Yet the church is simultaneously criticized by its foes for being against homosexual acts and for failing to act strongly enough against such acts, committed against its own code, by a minority of its own priests. There is a whiff of having it both ways here.

State-run homes for children have no doubt had their share of sexual abuse, but this has never been used as an argument against the existence of the state, nor would it be a very good argument if it were.

The use of this claim that religious instruction is a form of child abuse in an argument for atheism is propaganda, not reason. It is, as John Henry Newman once said of Charles Kingsley, "poisoning the wells." We read to the young, show them beautiful things, introduce them to good manners, warn them against dangers, teach them their letters and multiplication tables, and make them learn poetry by heart, precisely because they are most impressionable in childhood — and therefore best able to learn these things then, in many cases long before they can possibly understand why they matter. In the same way, we warn them against various dangers that they cannot possibly understand. It is also true, as I think most observant parents know, that children are much more interested in the universe and the fundamental questions of existence than are adults.

So this is the moment at which we try to pass on to them our deepest beliefs, and the moment when they are most likely to receive them. As Philip Pullman has rightly said, "'Once upon a time ...' is always a more effective instructor than 'Thou Shalt Not ...,'" so we do this most effectively with stories. But if we ourselves believe — and are asked by our own children what we believe — we will tell them, and they will instantly know if we mean it and also know how much it matters to us. They will learn from this that belief is a good thing. We will also try to find schools that will at the very least not undermine the morals and faith of the home. And for this, we are to be called abusers of children? This has the stench of totalitarian slander, paving the road to suppression and persecution.

By contrast, I say unequivocally that if a man wishes to bring his child up as an atheist, he should be absolutely free to do so. I am confident enough of the rightness of Christianity to believe that such a child may well learn later (though with more difficulty than he deserves) that he has been misled. But it is ridiculous to pretend that it is a neutral act to inform an infant that the heavens are empty, that the universe is founded on chaos rather than love, and that his grandparents, on dying, have ceased altogether to exist. I personally think it wrong to tell children such things, because I believe them to be false and wrong and roads to misery of various kinds. But in a free country, parents should be able to do so. In return, I ask for the same consideration for religious parents.

However, the new anti-theism is emphatically not just an opinion seeking its place in a plural society. It is a dogmatic tyranny in the making. I can see no purpose in the suggestion that religion is itself child abuse, apart from an attempt by atheists to create the atmosphere in which religious instruction of children can be regulated and perhaps prevented by law.

The Totalitarian Intolerance of the New Atheists

This is not speculation on my part. Professor Dawkins is surprisingly explicit about his own intolerance. He returned to the same theme in an article entitled "Religion's Real Child Abuse."[11] In this he provided a strong clue to his own convictions when he enthusiastically advertised an astonishing lecture delivered by a man he plainly regards with approval. Dawkins writes:

> "What shall we tell the children?" is a superb polemic on how religions abuse the minds of children, by the distinguished psychologist Nicholas Humphrey. It was originally delivered as a lecture in aid of Amnesty International, and has now been reissued as a chapter of his book, *The Mind Made Flesh*, just published by Oxford University Press. It is also available on the worldwide web and I strongly rec-

---

11. Published on "RichardDawkins.net" on May 15, 2006.

ommend it.[12] Humphrey argues that, in the same way as Amnesty works tirelessly to free political prisoners the world over, we should work to free the children of the world from the religions which, with parental approval, damage minds too young to understand what is happening to them. He is right, and the same lesson should inform our discussions of the current paedophile brouhaha. Priestly groping of child bodies is disgusting. But it may be less harmful in the long run than priestly subversion of child minds.

Turning to Mr. Humphrey's lecture, we find the standard introduction always given by those who demand a restriction on freedom of speech. That is, he proclaims his strong support for freedom of speech, except in this one little case:

Freedom of speech is too precious a freedom to be meddled with. And however painful some of its consequences may sometimes be for some people, we should still as a matter of principle resist putting curbs on it. By all means we should try to make up for the harm that other people's words do, but not by censoring the words as such.

And, since I am so sure of this in general, and since I'd expect most of you to be so too, I shall probably shock you when I say it is the purpose of my lecture tonight to argue in one particular area just the opposite. To argue, in short, in favour of censorship, against freedom of expression, and to do so moreover in an area of life that has traditionally been regarded as sacrosanct.

I am talking about moral and religious education. And

---

12. I recommend it as well, but for different reasons.

especially the education a child receives at home, where parents are allowed — even expected — to determine for their children what counts as truth and falsehood, right and wrong. Children, I'll argue, have a human right not to have their minds crippled by exposure to other people's bad ideas — no matter *who* these other people are.

Parents, correspondingly, have no god-given licence to enculturate their children in whatever ways they personally choose: no right to limit the horizons of their children's knowledge, to bring them up in an atmosphere of dogma and superstition, or to insist they follow the straight and narrow paths of their own faith. In short, children have a right not to have their minds addled by nonsense. And we as a society have a duty to protect them from it. So we should no more allow parents to teach their children to believe, for example, in the literal truth of the Bible, or that the planets rule their lives, than we should allow parents to knock their children's teeth out or lock them in a dungeon. That's the negative side of what I want to say. But there will be a positive side as well. If children have a right to be protected from false ideas, they have too a right to be succoured by the truth. And we as a society have a duty to provide it. Therefore we should feel as much obliged to pass on to our children the best scientific and philosophical understanding of the natural world — to teach, for example, the truths of evolution and cosmology, or the methods.[13]

Like all repressive arguments advanced by supposedly liberal minds, this one is repellently slippery. Note how moral and reli-

13. *The Mind Made Flesh: Essays from the Frontiers of Psychology and Evolution* (Oxford: Oxford University Press, 2003), 291.

gious education are immediately characterized as dogma and superstition, dismissed automatically as "narrow." Note how Bible literalism is assumed and then equated with astrology. Note how a few words later this is bracketed with the knocking out of teeth and imprisonment in a dungeon. Note the assertion that those ideas he disapproves are "false."

Further on in the same diatribe come the other confusions so beloved of the anti-theist front. Before we know where we are, the guilt-by-association smear has been deployed once again and we are on to female genital mutilation and alleged censorship:

> Let's suppose indeed that this is a lecture about female circumcision. And the issue is not whether anyone should be permitted to deny a girl knowledge of Darwin, but whether anyone should be permitted to deny her the uses of a clitoris. And now here I am suggesting that it is a girl's right to be left intact, that parents have no right to mutilate their daughters to suit their own socio-sexual agenda, and that we as a society ought to prevent it. What's more, to make the positive case as well, that every girl should actually be encouraged to find out how best to use to her own advantage the intact body she was born with.

First, the suggestion seems to be that religious people support genital mutilation. Then such mutilation is equated with denials of the knowledge of Darwin — which Christians do not seek to bring about smear upon smear upon smear.

I cannot reproduce the whole monstrous thing here (it is readily available through two clicks of a computer mouse), but

I feel I should reproduce Humphrey's attempt to counter the doubts that some of his audience might have.

> "Let me catch the question from the back of the hall, which I imagine goes something like this: "How'd you like it if some Big Brother were to insist on your children being taught his beliefs? How'd you like it if I tried to impose my personal ideology on your little girl?" I have the answer: that teaching science isn't like that, it's not about teaching someone else's beliefs, it's about encouraging the child to exercise her powers of understanding to arrive at her own beliefs."[14]

So there. His belief, as my brother also insists, is not a belief. He is not Big Brother. That is some other person. How can we know? It is just the blindingly obvious truth. So why can't you see it, you unteachable moron? Which has been the starting point of the secret policeman and the Inquisition merchant (see, I'm against the Spanish Inquisition, too, as any English schoolboy reared on tales of Drake and Raleigh and Grenville must be) down all the centuries.

Fearing God and Nothing Else

Which brings me neatly back to the Soviet state, which also crushed liberty of thought in the name of enlightenment. In answering the question, "Why did the Soviet state not compromise with religion?" I must also challenge the linked idea that the worship of human power is identical to the worship of almighty God. This is often stated by my brother, who claims

---

14. Ibid., 316.

that North Korea's leader worship is identical to religion, except that "at least you can die in North Korea." How does it differ? Quite fundamentally.

Roger Scruton, commenting on Maximilien Robespierre's bizarre Festival of the Supreme Being, remarked that the "supreme Being" seemed to be conveniently similar to Robespierre's idea of the Revolution in its character and demands — whereas the Christian is "answerable for his soul to God and to no earthly master."[15] Edmund Burke similarly once said that one who truly feared God (admittedly quite a difficult thing to do) feared nothing and nobody else. At least you can get to heaven from a North Korean labor camp or torture chamber. You may also be able to arrive in hell from a North Korean palace. And if you believe that, then the Great Leader has no power to control you. According to the believer, God's commandments and requirements exist outside time and cannot be amended even by Kim Il Sung. If we love the thing that God commands and desire the things he promises, then we too can live outside time and beyond the reach of Stalin, Kim, Mao, Pol Pot, Hitler, or the rest — as their dungeons prove.

Even unbelievers have to recognize that God, whether he exists or not, predates earthly dictators and tends to survive them. God's laws and Christian morals do the same. If God is not dethroned and his laws not revoked, he represents an important rival to the despot's authority, living in millions of hearts. If he cannot be driven out of hearts, total control by the state is impossible. This may seem trivial to us in our secularized societies still benefiting from the freedoms that flowed from

15. *The Times*, London, 10 July, 1989. See www.alor.org/Britain/... and www .vanguardnewsnetwork.com/letters/100304letters.htm.

centuries of Christianity. We have forgotten how we arrived at our civilized state. Religion has retreated to far fringes of daily life, and death, its great ally, is hidden behind screens. But it was certainly not so for the Russian revolutionaries or Western European Marxists, who recognized early on that there would be no equivalent of the Bolshevik takeover in Germany, France, Italy, or Britain — because the peoples of the European continent, well-informed about revolution, were too much in love with Christianity, liberty, and legality to believe in any utopia.

Robespierre disagreed with his fellow revolutionaries about how to replace the church, and it is arguable that they murdered him in case he began to think that he was himself God. By doing so, they murdered the French Revolution, since Robespierre embodied the state. Thus the state, being all-powerful and vested in him, could not survive his death. But Robespierre, being mortal, did not rise again, nor did the French Revolution, which has been worshiped in theory and ignored in practice ever since by Frenchmen who know only too well what "Liberty, Equality, and Fraternity" really mean in practice. The more ordinary Jacobins — especially Jacques Hebert and Joseph Fouche — wanted to extirpate religion while they reinvented the world as a kingdom of decimalized reason, in which everything could be divided by the number of toes a man has, and in which God did not exist because he could not be divided by ten or charted by an astrolabe. Both Hebert and Fouche demonstrated in bloody practice that they believed that laws were dead, humans were mammals rather than made in the image of God (and so expendable), and man was in a state of nature where he could do what he liked in the name of the revolution.

It is clear from the history of Soviet persecution of Christianity that the Bolsheviks were extirpators too. Stalin was certainly a new Tsar, in that he was all-powerful and the foundation of the state. But he could not be a new God, because the revolution had deliberately killed God and made any other deity impossible — thoroughly and intentionally. So when Stalin died in 1953, that state had nothing but force and fear, sausage, vodka, medals, and wartime patriotism to keep it alive. And when the force failed and the fear weakened, and the sausage and the vodka ran out, and nobody wanted medals any more, that state died. Since its failure, attempts to rebuild it as a proper civil society have failed. There are many reasons for its descent into crude autocracy, its continuing reliance on the Lenin cult, and the prevalence of organized crime, drunken disorder, universal dishonesty, cultural decay, devastated family life, and corruption. But one of the most important must be the absence of conscience and self-restraint among even its educated people, and the vacuum where the rule of law ought to be.

The League of the Militant Godless had done their work too well. In the names of reason, science, and liberty they had proved, rather effectively, that good societies need God to survive and that when you have murdered him, starved him, silenced him, denied him to the children, and erased his festivals and his memory, you have a gap that cannot indefinitely be filled by any human, nor anything made by human hands.

Must we discover this all over again? I fear so. A new and intolerant utopianism seeks to drive the remaining traces of Christianity from the laws and constitutions of Europe and North America. This time, it does so mainly in the cause of personal liberation, born in the 1960s cultural revolution, and now inflamed into special rage by any suggestion that the sexual urge should be restrained by moral limits or that it should have any necessary connection with procreation. This utopianism relies for human goodness on doctrines of human rights derived from human desires and — like all such codes — full of conflicts between the differing rights of different groups. These must then be policed by an ever more powerful state. A new elite, wealthy and comfortable beyond the fantasies of any previous generation, abandons penal codes (especially against the possession of narcotics) and abolishes marital fidelity so as to license its own comfortable, padded indulgence, and it therefore permits the same freedoms to the poor, who suffer far more from this dangerous liberty than do the rich.

Inevitably, it is the Christian churches who are the last strongholds of resistance to this change. Yet they are historically weak, themselves infiltrated by secular liberalism, full of uncertainty and diffidence. The overthrow of Christian education is a real possibility in our generation. The removal of Christianity from broadcasting and public ceremonies is almost complete. Expressions of Christian opinion or prayer in public premises can be punished in Britain under new codes that enjoin a post-Christian code of "equality and diversity" on all public servants. Secularists are equating the teaching of religion with child abuse and laying the foundations for it to be restricted by law. Britain's next monarch is likely to be crowned in a multi-faith ceremony whose main significance will be that it will be the first Coronation not to be explicitly Christian in more than a thousand years. The Rage against God is loose and is preparing to strip the remaining altars when it is strong enough.

Epilogue

I end this book in Grand Rapids, Michigan, with some thoughts on the unsatisfactory debate that I had there in April 2008, with my brother Christopher, about the existence of God and the goodness of religion. I had decided before it took place that I would not take part in such a debate again, on this or any other subject.

Christopher and I have had over the past fifty years what might be called a difficult relationship. Some brothers get along; some do not. We were the sort who just didn't. (Parents of such siblings will know about this.)

Who knows why? At one stage — I was about nine, he nearly twelve — my poor gentle father actually persuaded us to sign a peace treaty in the hope of halting our feud. I can still picture this doomed pact in its red frame, briefly hanging on the wall. To my shame, I was the one who repudiated it, ripped it from its frame, and angrily erased my signature before recommencing hostilities. In a way, the treaty has remained broken ever since, and heaven knows what happened to the sad little document.

On that Thursday night in Grand Rapids, however, the old quarrel was—as far as I am concerned—finished for good, whatever it was about. Just at the point where many might have expected—and some might have hoped—that we would rend and tear at each other, we did not. Both of us, I suspect, recoiled from such an exhibition, which might have been amusing for others, because we were brothers—but would have been wrong, because we are brothers.

I had already concluded, as my train nosed westward in the spring twilight through the lovely, wistful mountain and river country that lies between Harper's Ferry and Pittsburgh, that I did not want to do anything of the kind. Normally I love to argue in front of audiences. This time I seemed to have no taste for it.

Something far more important than a debate had happened a few days before, when Christopher and I had met in his apartment in Washington, D.C. If he despised and loathed me for my Christian beliefs, he wasn't showing it. We were more than civil, treating each other as equals—and as brothers with a common childhood, even recalling bicycle rides we used to take together on summer days in the Sussex Downs, unimaginably long ago, which I did not even realize he still remembered. And here is another thing. When our Grand Rapids hosts chose the date of April 3 for this debate, they had no way of knowing that it was the sixty-third anniversary of our parents' wedding—an optimistic, happy day in the last weeks of what had been for both of them a fairly grim war. Not all the optimism was justified, and with the blessed hindsight of parenthood, I cannot imagine that our long fraternal squabble did much for their later happiness. They are, alas, long gone, but my brother and I had both independently become a little concerned at how we should conduct ourselves on such a day.

We had each reached the conclusion, unbidden, that we did not want this to turn into a regular traveling circus, becoming steadily more phony as it progressed around the circuit.

Perhaps I had begun to suspect that something had shifted during our evening in Washington. To my open astonishment, Christopher even cooked supper, a domesticated action so unexpected that I still haven't got over it. It would be almost as unsettling to come across Mick Jagger living in a Florida retirement community or President Obama attending a meeting of the National Rifle Association. If Christopher is going to take up roasting legs of lamb at this stage in his life, then what else might be possible?

My brother had even given up smoking — a man who once smoked so much, so intensely and with such incessant dedication that one observer wondered if he was doing it simply to keep warm. I am not hoping for a late conversion because he has won a successful battle against cigarettes. He has bricked himself up high in his atheist tower, with slits instead of windows from which to shoot arrows at the faithful, and he would find it rather hard to climb down out of it. But I have the more modest hope that he might one day arrive at some sort of acceptance that belief in God is not necessarily a character fault — and that religion does not poison everything. Beyond that, I can only say that those who choose to argue in prose, even if it is very good prose, are unlikely to be receptive to a case that is most effectively couched in poetry.

Christopher and I had been in public arguments before. We had had the occasional clash on TV or radio. We had debated the legacy of the Sixties, in a more evenly matched encounter than Grand Rapids, eleven years earlier in London. Not long after that, there had been a long, unrewarding falling-out over something I had said about politics. Both of us were urged by others to end this quarrel and eventually, if rather tentatively, did so.

When I attacked his book against God, some people seemed almost to hope that our personal public squabble would begin again. No doubt they would have been pleased or entertained if we had pelted each other with slime in Grand Rapids. But despite one or two low blows exchanged in the heat of the moment, I do not think we did much to satisfy them. I hope not. At the end I concluded that, while the audience perhaps had not noticed, we had ended the evening on better terms than either of us might have expected. This was — and remains — more important to me than the debate itself.

So I will say this. On this my brother and I agree: that independence of mind is immensely precious, and that we should try to tell the truth in clear English even if we are disliked for doing so. Oddly enough this leads us, in many things, to be far closer than most people think we are on some questions — closer, sometimes, than we would particularly wish to be. The same paradox sometimes also makes us arrive at different conclusions from very similar arguments, which is easier than it might appear. This will not make us close friends at this stage. We are two utterly different men approaching the ends of two intensely separate lives. Let us not be sentimental here, nor rashly over-optimistic.

But I was astonished, on that spring evening by the Grand River, to find that — in the middle of what was supposed to be a ruthless, jeering clash of opposed minds — the longest quarrel of my life seemed unexpectedly to be over, so many years and so many thousands of miles after it had started, in our quiet homes and our first beginnings in an England now impossibly remote from us. It may actually be true, as I have long hoped it would be, that "the end of all our exploring will be to arrive where we started and know the place for the first time."

Acknowledgments

I am neither a theologian nor even a Bible scholar. Nor am I a philosopher, nor a "public intellectual," whatever that may be. I don't think I am even an intellectual in private, just a jobbing newspaper scribbler who has spent more than thirty years in the University of Fleet Street.

I never had any illusions about the blunt purpose of this book. My only qualification for writing it is that I am me, a former atheist with some skill at words who has returned to the Church and whose brother is in the vanguard of the current attack on religion. I took some convincing that this was enough. So I must above all record my thanks to Sandra Vander Zicht, associate publisher and executive editor at Zondervan, who doggedly persuaded me to take on the task, endured my repeated attacks of doubt and pessimism, and then with skill and patience helped to shape my arguments and recollections into a coherent whole.

Particular thanks should also go to my elder son, Daniel, without whom I don't think this work would have been finished, and whose encouragement and advice were invaluable. Anthony McCarthy also gave me vital advice and assistance at many stages. My wife, Eve, provided, as she always has, indispensable companionship, support, and comfort.

If there is any credit, they should share in it. If there is any blame, it rests with me.

PJH
Oxford
January 2010

Index